The Thirty-six Immortal Women Poets

The Thirty-six Immortal Women Poets

A poetry album
with illustrations by Chōbunsai Eishi

Introduction, Commentaries,
and Translations
by Andrew J. Pekarik

BARRIE & JENKINS
LONDON

Acknowledgments

I would like to thank Haruo Shirane for his comments on a draft of the translations and commentaries, and Mrs. Yoshiko Ushioda, Curator, for her transcription of the preface from the version of Eishi's album in The Chester Beatty Collection, Dublin. My special thanks to Hiroshi Onishi for his help in reading and translating the preface and afterwords of the album, and to my editor, Adrienne Baxter, for her dedicated and expert assistance in every stage of this project.

Andrew J. Pekarik

First published in Great Britain in 1991 by Barrie & Jenkins Ltd, 20 Vauxhall Bridge Road, London SW1V 2SA

Reproduced from the volume *Nishikizuri onna sanjūrokkasen* in The Spencer Collection, The New York Public Library, Astor, Lenox, and Tilden Foundations.

A catalogue record for this book is available from the British Library.

ISBN 0 7126 5008 3

Title page illustration: Daini no sanmi, the daughter of Murasaki Shikibu, from the album of The Thirty-six Immortal Women Poets in Colour Prints by Chōbunsai Eishi in The Spencer Collection of The New York Public Library.

This volume was designed by Heidi Haeuser/Abby Goldstein Design Studio, New York. Photography by Philip Pocock. The paper is 140 gsm Colorit Creamy woodfree (mfg. Sweden). The text and display are typeset in Bembo by U.S. Lithograph, typographers. Printed and bound by Mandarin Offset, Hong Kong.

First edition

Contents

Introduction

The Album

This volume reproduces a woodblock-printed album in the Spencer Collection of The New York Public Library. The album, entitled *Nishikizuri onna sanjūrokkasen* (The Thirty-six Immortal Women Poets in Color Prints), was published by Eijudō Nishimuraya Yohachi in Edo (Tokyo) in 1801 as a deluxe album of thirty-six color prints, each showing a poet on the left and one of her poems on the right, with a frontispiece by Hokusai, a preface in Japanese (missing from the Spencer Collection copy), two afterwords in Chinese, one in Japanese, and finally a colophon (also missing in this album). The illustrations of the poets were designed by Hosoda (Chōbunsai) Eishi (1756–1829), and the poems were reproduced in calligraphy in 1797 by thirty-six girls between the ages of six and fifteen.

Although we are now more struck by its colorful illustrations, the album originally functioned as a publicity vehicle to show off the accomplishments of the young girls whose calligraphy records the poems. On the right-hand margin of each page is a small note recording the address, name, and age of the child responsible. For example, the poem by Ukon (5L) was copied by Toyota Mine, age six, and the poem by Michitsuna no haha (6L) was brushed by the girl's ten-year-old sister, Toyota Ito.* The children were all pupils of Hanagata Yoshiakira, who ran a calligraphy school called Hanagata shodō, and who sponsored the publication. The purpose of the album was probably either to solicit new students or to serve as a model book. According to an advertisement that accompanies the colophon, a complimentary illustrated text of thirty-six poets with calligraphy by male students was also planned. The boys never had their chance for fame, however, as the book was not published.

The album works well as advertisement. The calligraphy looks completely professional and remarkably uniform, a feature that may owe something to the models that the children were probably copying and to the skill of the woodblock carvers (recorded in the colophon as Yamaguchi Matsugorō and Yamaguchi Kiyozō), who would have cleaned up any rough spots when they cut the blocks.

In order to demonstrate that the training of these young girls went beyond simple skill in drawing *kana* (the elements of Japanese syllabic script), they were called on to transcribe the poems within an unusually broad range of formats—from regular even lines to complex scatterings of syllables that almost require a map in order to be read. By embracing this variety, the sponsors could imply that the children not only are learning to write with surprising facility, but also are learning the aesthetics of calligraphy and the fundamental principles of poetry. This would be a compelling attraction to their affluent parents, who would like to

---

* for a note on the references 5L and 6L, please see page 192

see their offspring introduced to the world of classical Japanese culture.

The poets and poems in this album were already part of the distant past in Japan when the work was published. Over five hundred years separated the time of the latest poet represented from the young girls and their calligraphy teachers. The style of dress shown in the illustrations was still worn by only a few nobles in Kyoto for ceremonial occasions. The language of the poetry was already remote and sometimes obscure, and it is doubtful that the girls fully understood what they were copying.

For the public at the start of the nineteenth century, this book was an inexpensive classic, an affordable version of the hand-painted and richly decorated scrolls and albums from the golden age of court society that were still preserved as treasures in the storehouses of the great aristocrats. Now, nearly two hundred years later, it is being made yet more widely available to a new audience.

The poets included in the album were active during the Heian (794–1185) and Kamakura (1185–1333) periods, from the ninth century through the mid-thirteenth century. During this time the imperial court in Kyoto was the center of an extraordinarily sophisticated culture that held poetry in the highest regard, though it was also justifiably proud of its accomplishments in calligraphy, music, dance, and painting. Even in the Edo period (1615–1868), when emperors were virtually powerless and court poetry was no more than a sterile repetition of the past, this aristocratic culture remained the central symbol of Japan's artistic accomplishment and identity.

In the long period between the thirteenth and the nineteenth centuries, the literary culture of the Heian and Kamakura periods was mostly preserved by the descendants of the old aristocratic families who hand-copied the ancient texts and passed on the study of poetry to a few select students. Knowledge of the classics began to spread more widely only in the seventeenth century, when printed versions of the anthologies were produced and as the class distinctions limiting the study of old poetry broke down.

The thirty-six poems that form the text of this album are not a casual collection of famous verse. Both the poets and the poems had been carefully selected and arranged many centuries before the album was created. This specific group of "Thirty-six Immortal Women Poets" was first determined in the second half of the thirteenth century. We do not know who created the list, but it was directly inspired by a small anthology, made in the early eleventh century by the court poet Fujiwara no Kintō (966–1041), called *Sanjūrokunin sen* (Selection of Thirty-six Poets).

Kintō, a contemporary of Murasaki Shikibu, author of *The Tale of Genji,* was the leading poetry critic of his time. He is said to have been involved in a dispute with Prince Tomohira (964–1009) over who was the greater poet, Kakinomoto no Hitomaro or Ki no Tsurayuki. Hitomaro was the major poet in the first important anthology of Japanese verse, the *Man'yōshū* (Collection of Myriad Leaves), assembled in the eighth century. Tsurayuki was the principal compiler of the *Kokin wakashū* (Collection of Japanese Poems from Ancient and Modern Times), completed around 905 and the first anthology of Japanese poetry assembled on the command of an emperor. Both poets were giants of the court poetry tradition and Hitomaro was even revered as a Shinto deity.

Kintō (favoring Tsurayuki) and Tomohira (backing Hitomaro) dealt with the problem of greatness by selecting ten poems by each poet and evaluating them against one another in pairs. Hitomaro won eight of the rounds, Tsurayuki one, and one was a tie.[1] This experience gave Kintō the idea of constructing the *Sanjūrokunin sen*, an imaginary competition between two teams, each with eighteen famous poets. One team, the Left Team, was led by Hitomaro, and the opposition, the Right Team, was led by Tsurayuki. Kintō selected three poems from the works of each poet and paired them against one another to suggest an actual poetry competition.

The poets in Kintō's selection became known as the "Thirty-six Immortal Poets."[2] Later critics imitated this approach with their own selections, such as the "Thirty-six Immortal Poets of the Heian Period," the "Thirty-six Immortal Buddhist Poets," and the "Thirty-six Immortal Women Poets." It seemed as if virtually any category could become a focus for an imaginary competition of thirty-six poets, and there are even surviving examples of imaginary poetry competitions with thirty-six craftsmen, or even with thirty-six insects.

Whoever first assembled the set of Thirty-six Immortal Women Poets had one other important inspiration besides the Thirty-six Immortal Poets. In 1235, over two hundred years after Kintō selected the Thirty-six, Retired Emperor Gotoba, who was himself an accomplished poet, carried the idea one step further by creating the *Jidai fudō utaawase* (Poetry Competition of Different Periods), an imaginary competition in which fifty poets from the tenth century and earlier faced off against fifty poets from the eleventh and twelfth centuries. This made the imaginary competition not only a comparison of individual poets, but also a contest between the older period and the more recent one.

These imaginary competitions did not originally include any judgments. Readers were encouraged to make their own determinations about who was the better poet, or which was the greater period for poetry. Comparisons of these poems could help poets to understand the tradition more clearly and to improve their own work.

We date the selection of "Thirty-six Immortal Women Poets" to the second half of the thirteenth century primarily because it does not include any poets active after that time. As in the case of Kintō's selection, it separates the poets into two teams and lists three poems for each poet.[3] And, as in Gotoba's imaginary competition, it separates the poets into a team of ancients and a team of moderns.

Different versions of the text correspond on the selection of the poets and their order (although there are a few exceptions that are obvious errors, as in Round 13 in this album), but they do not all include the same poems. Moreover, some texts, like this one, have only one poem per poet. The wide variety of poems selected for the many versions of this competition suggests that interested readers kept trying to improve it to suit their own preferences. Whoever put together the particular text used in this album was thoughtfully constructing a personal version of the competition. We have no way of determining when this compiler worked. It could have been anytime between 1250 and 1797.

As in most other works of this kind, the compiler's text may have been copied and recopied a number of times before it came into the hands of the calligraphy school and became the source for this album. Some poems differ slightly from their standard versions in major anthologies, but most of these variations are insignificant or are justified by other sources. There are two significant textual discrepancies unique to this album, however. One is in Round 16L, where the final line of the poem has been left out, and the other is in Round 12R, where the second half of the poem was replaced by the second half of a completely unrelated poem by another poet. This second mistake is so unusual and so unlikely that it is hard to imagine who might have been responsible for it. It certainly was not the compiler, who knew poetry too well to make such an error.

The album was bound soon after printing, but it was rebound at a later time, probably in the late nineteenth or early twentieth century. When the book was taken apart, the restorer did not number the pages (except for the last one), and when he put it back together again the order of pages was seriously confused. This reproduction reestablishes the original sequence of the poets as dictated by the earliest source material. After that rebinding and before it entered the Spencer Collection, the album accidentally lost its back cover, its colophon, and its Japanese preface, but none of the central pages was damaged.

The Poems

Women played a very important role in the development of Japanese poetry. Some of the oldest poems in the language were composed by women, such as Princess Nukada, who in the seventh century wrote the following:[4]

umasake	Though I would be looking back
miwa no yama	again and again upon Mount Miwa
aoniyoshi	of the delicious wine,
nara no yama no	Until it recedes
yama no ma ni	between the hills of Nara,
ikakuru made	beautiful in the blue earth,

michi no kuma	Until the bends in this road
itsumoru made ni	heap high,
tsubara ni mo	Though I would long
mitsutsu yukamu o	turn my distant gaze
shibashiba mo	upon that mountain,
misakemu yama o	Is it right that the clouds
kokoro naku	Should heartlessly conceal it?
kumo no	
kakusaubeshi ya	
hanka:	Envoy:
miwa yama o	Miwa Mountain.
shika mo kakusu ka	Do they hide it like this?
kumo dani mo	Would that clouds at least
kokoro arana mo	Had sympathy, for is it right
kakusaubeshi ya	That they should conceal it?

As this example indicates, some early Japanese poems comprised extended sequences of alternating measures of five and seven syllables, and are thus called *chōka* ("long poem"). They could extend beyond forty measures in some cases. They were usually followed by a separate short verse of five measures, called *hanka* ("envoy") or *tanka* ("short poem"), that responded to or summarized the content of the long poem. The five measures of the *tanka* contained five, seven, five, seven, and seven syllables respectively.

Many early long poems were closely linked to religious or ceremonial events. Some scholars, for example, think that Princess Nukada's poem was composed for a ceremony to pacify the spirit of Miwa Mountain on the occasion of moving the capital.[5] Certainly the extended, stately language of these long poems combines a sense of incantation and procession. The master of the *chōka* was the late-seventh-century court poet Kakinomoto no Hitomaro.

The long form did not continue to interest poets. By the beginning of the Heian period, the *chōka* was in a decline from which it never recovered, and almost all Japanese poems were written in the five-measure *tanka* form. The *tanka*, which was most often simply called *waka* ("Japanese poem"), was principally defined by its meter. A series of words could be considered a poem only if they could be divided into five measures (called *ku*, "phrases"). Each measure was one or more words, with five, seven, five, seven, and seven syllables respectively. The metrical structure was usually not visible, however, when the poem was written. Calligraphers had many different and creative approaches to recording poetry; the most obvious, division into five lines, was only one, and a rare one at that.

The five measures of a *waka* were seen as constituting two sections. The first three measures (five-seven-five syllables) was the upper part (*kami no ku*, "upper measures"), and the final two measures (seven-seven) formed the lower part (*shimo no ku*, "lower measures"). Calligraphers frequently wrote poems in two lines, corresponding to these two parts.

Poems were often shared orally, and the thirty-one-syllable metrical structure was very important in these presentations. In a fictional diary, *Tosa nikki* (A Tosa Journal), written by Tsurayuki in 935 or 936, we are told of a session of relaxed poetry making:

> After listening intently to the comments on the poems, a certain person produced one that proved to contain thirty-seven syllables. To his indignation, everyone burst out laughing. One would try in vain to recite such a poem. Even if it were written down, it would be impossible to read. Since it was so difficult on the very day of its composition, imagine what it would be like later![6]

We do not know precisely how ancient Japanese recited their poems. On some occasions, they were sung to musical accompaniment, or chanted (as they still are in Tokyo today, at the annual poetry presentation in the imperial palace). Whatever the method of recitation, standard vocalization patterns based on meter announced the presence of poetic form, and thus were of fundamental importance in the very definition of a poem.

In this volume, we have chosen to arrange the Japanese poems on the page in five lines corresponding to the five measures of the *waka*; their translations approximate that form as well, in order to emphasize the significance of the metrical structure, and to allow translations to make use of the powerful technique of lineation that is so central to poetry in English.

The thirty-one-syllable form was essential to the idea of the *waka*; it also had a critical influence on the development and uses of poetry. The metrical rule is so simple that poetic composition was, at least theoretically, within reach of just about anyone who could count or follow the recitation form. Many poems, even by well-known poets, are simple, grammatical statements in ordinary language virtually indistinguishable from prose, except that they conform to the required meter. As a result, it was possible for people to compose acceptable poetry casually on social occasions without too much training or literary ability. Even conversational exchanges were possible in verse.

At the same time, the thirty-one-syllable *waka* was so short that it was a serious challenge for skilled poets. Each word and grammatical particle had to matter. The structures of these small verses often became remarkably complex as professionals manipulated grammar and meaning with inversions, omissions, and special rhetorical techniques. Classical Japanese language is notably ambiguous to begin with, but when it is deliberately pushed by double meanings, abbreviated grammar, and uncertain references, it becomes, in many cases, eloquently obscure.

There are often alternative interpretations for even the most basic sense of a poem, and the poets did not shy away from these possibilities. They expected that the experience of each poem would be relatively open-ended, influenced by the knowledge and background of the reader, and shaped by the context in which it was received. Many of the poems in this book, for example, were originally presented as personal exchanges. The people who sent or recited them and the people who first received or heard them knew one another at least indirectly, and had a private history within which the poem resonated in a way that we can never hope to recover.

Poets also composed for posterity, and their words were recorded both by themselves in personal journals and by others. In their later years poets (or their admirers) often created anthologies of their works by selecting their best compositions and recording them together with the poems that inspired or answered them. It became standard practice to precede a poem with a brief headnote that described the original circumstance of composition.

Poets realized that assembling poems with headnotes in anthologies—positioning them in new contexts—was itself an artistic act in which poems could be reexperienced in interesting ways. The first great anthology of Japanese poetry, the *Man'yōshū*, is, in fact, an anthology of anthologies containing poems (both *chōka* and *waka*) from the earliest times to the eighth century. Its volumes include many different systems of arrangement, incorporating those based on chronology and those based on critical categories.

The methods for organizing short poems into long anthologies became extraordinarily sophisticated as the court tradition of *waka* composition and criticism developed. By the thirteenth century, it seemed that poets were as determined to fit their works smoothly into the elaborate structures of anthologies as they were to compose compelling expressions of feeling.

In both composition and arrangement, the standards for the court *waka* were set by the twenty-one imperial anthologies compiled between 905 and 1439 that formed the mainstream and canon of the Japanese poetry tradition. Each of these anthologies was ordered by an emperor who summoned one or more of the leading poets of the time to assemble them. They vary in quality, since some emperors cared more and since some compilers had factional or critical preferences that colored their choices. But for anyone who ever wrote a poem in court circles, to be included in one of these anthologies was to be recognized as a poet and immortalized.

The first and most important imperial anthology was the *Kokin wakashū*. Its largest and most important sections contain seasonal poems (on spring, summer, autumn, and winter), and love poems. Seasonal and love poetry dominated all later imperial anthologies as well. Within each of these categories, poems were arranged in roughly chronological sequence, with the first poems describing the beginning of a season or affair, and the last poems the end.

All of the poems in this album previously appeared in imperial anthologies, sometimes centuries after they were composed. In many cases the anthologies provide headnotes describing the original circumstances of their composition, but these notes were not incorporated into this imaginary poetry competition. The poems in the album are each included in one of the following imperial anthologies (cited with the date each was compiled, the usual abbreviation for the anthology, and the number of poems represented in this album):[7]

1. *Kokin wakashū* (Collection of Japanese Poems from Ancient and Modern Times). ca. 905. (KKS) Two poems.

2. *Gosen wakashū* (Later Collection of Japanese Poems). ca. 951. (GSS) Two poems.

4. *Goshūi wakashū* (Later Collection of Gleanings of Japanese Poems). 1086. (GSIS) Five poems.

5. *Kin'yō wakashū* (Golden Leaves Collection of Japanese Poems). ca. 1127. (KYS) One poem.

7. *Senzai wakashū* (Thousand Years Collection of Japanese Poems). 1188. (SZS) Four poems.

8. *Shinkokin wakashū* (New Collection of Japanese Poems from Ancient and Modern Times). 1206. (SKKS) Thirteen poems.

10. *Shokugosen wakashū* (Later Collection of Japanese Poems, Continued). 1251. (ShokuGSS) Four poems.

11. *Shokukokin wakashū* (Collection of Japanese Poems from Ancient and Modern Times, Continued). 1265. (ShokuKKS) Four poems.

14. *Gyokuyō wakashū* (Jeweled Leaves Collection of Japanese Poems). 1313 or 1314. (GYS) One poem.

Although the poems in the imperial anthologies are generally of high quality, they are certainly not all masterpieces. Some were included to maintain smooth connections within the arrangement of poems in a section, or because their authors were too powerful to ignore; others were deliberately meant to provide modest backgrounds for the outstanding poems that were set like jewels among them. The compiler of the imaginary poetry competition in this album was less concerned with the quality of individual poems than with how they would work together in a competition that contrasts women poets of different times.

By noting the total number of poems that each poet has in the twenty-one imperial anthologies, we can get a rough sense of the relative position of the poets within the mainstream tradition as a whole. On this basis we can say that Izumi Shikibu (240), Ise (178),

Princess Shikishi (154), Shunzei no musume (109), and Sagami (108) are the major figures. Ono no Komachi must be added to this list, although only a small number of her poems survive.[8]

It is no coincidence that all six of these poets were especially renowned for their love poems. Love poetry was considered to be something of a specialty of women poets, for reasons both historical and social.

Historically women played a key role in composing Japanese poetry, especially when it was threatened by a fashion for Chinese poetry at court. From the seventh century, Japan's ruling aristocracy made a prolonged and detailed effort to adopt key ideas and practices from China. Court rituals, offices, and dress, the placement and organization of cities, the ranks and titles of the nobility, the language of government business, and even the fundamental relationship between the emperor and his government and people, were all based on the study of Chinese models. The extent and intensity of this influence ebbed and flowed over the centuries, depending on the particular ruler, the political and international situation, and the relative maturity or vulnerability of institutions and practices.

In the writing of literature, the study of Chinese poetry sometimes created an enriching atmosphere that helped Japanese poetry to mature more rapidly, though sometimes it held it back. In the period covered by the *Man'yōshū*, Japanese poetry benefited by being recognized and appreciated as an independent artistic form with a secular value. Chinese poetry offered models for themes, approaches, and even techniques, such as intricate parallelisms. And as long as poets like Hitomaro wrote for court occasions, Japanese poetry served an important role in public life.

The first emperor of the Heian period, Kammu (737–806; r. 781–806), was a man of action who established the capital in Heian (Kyoto) and orchestrated military campaigns against tribes in the north who were not yet under the central authority of the court. He had some fondness for *waka*, as this incident from the history of his reign indicates:

> On the fourteenth day of the Fourth Month of the fourteenth year of Enryaku [795] a small banquet was given. The emperor sang the old song:
>
> | inishie no | The old path |
> | no naka furumichi | That runs through ancient fields— |
> | aratameba | When you change, |
> | aratamaramu ya | Will it too be changed? |
> | no naka furumichi | The old path through the fields. |

He ordered the female attendant, junior third rank Kudaraō Akinobu, to compose a response. She was unable to do so. The emperor himself replied in her stead:

kimi koso wa	You are the one
wasuretarurame	Who is likely to forget.
nigitama no	I, the graceful one,
tawayame ware wa	With gentle soul, am
tsune no shiratama	The pearl of eternity.

The courtiers all called out, "Long live the emperor!"[9]

Kammu was obviously very proficient at amorous exchanges in *waka*, which probably was a useful skill in his everyday life since he sired no less than thirty-five children by twenty different women.[10]

But the next important emperor, Kammu's son Saga (786–842; r. 809–823), was a fervent Sinophile who worked hard to reestablish the trappings of Chinese culture and ideas at the Heian court. Since there was no native writing system, Chinese was the written language of government, and all male members of the upper-level nobility learned to read and write Chinese. Saga insisted that they enter the university and study Chinese literature seriously. He was himself a prolific poet in Chinese, ordered the composition of *kanshi* ("Chinese poems") at major court events, and sponsored three anthologies of Chinese poetry.

During this so-called "Dark Age of the Public Waka,"[11] which centered on Saga's lifetime, Japanese poetry virtually disappeared from the court. Still, it continued to be used in amorous exchanges between men and women, and it was the lovers who kept the tradition alive in private until it could be reestablished in public.

Social conditions fostered such private exchanges. Women of the nobility were kept isolated in their homes, and courtship consisted of secret visits by the man to the woman's home. These secret visits were usually abetted by some member of the woman's household and may have been preceded by some slight or accidental contact. Many of the affairs described in *The Tale of Genji*, for example, begin with a passing glimpse of a man or woman that, due to the restrictions on contact between the sexes, quickly escalates into burning desire.

Marriage was usually relatively simple. After three consecutive nights together the union was made public and acknowledged by the family of the woman, but she continued to live where she had before, and her new husband continued to visit her and their children. The custom was so strong in the late seventh century, for example, that officials assigned to distant provinces were forbidden to take along their wives.[12] Separate residences for married couples began to end only in the mid-Heian period.[13]

Living apart is a strong motivation for messages of love. Moreover, men were not limited to one wife but often had several, who were visited independently and had to be consoled when they were left alone. Women also had opportunities for multiple affairs. Out of these circumstances eventually evolved the basic pattern of love exchanges: the man's courtship, the woman's resistance, the joy of meeting, the pain of waiting, the sorrow of parting, the woman's fear of rumor and abandonment, the man's protestation of good intentions, the woman's anger and resentment because of his neglect, and the final despair and sadness of both man and woman.

Women were not taught Chinese, so when it came to private exchanges of this kind, men had no alternative but to compose Japanese verse that could be presented in person or delivered by messenger. The *waka* was perfect for this purpose. It was easy to create, did not require elaborate structure or unusual language, and, because it was so short, was naturally both lyrical and open-ended.

In the ninth century, a new system for writing Japanese encouraged such exchanges between men and women. Simplified, cursive forms of Chinese characters were assigned phonetic values corresponding to syllables of Japanese. These forms, called *kana*, were easy to remember and write, were elegant, and required no knowledge of Chinese. Women quickly became proficient in *kana* calligraphy, and devoted messengers rushed back and forth across the capital carrying letters and poems of love—early in the morning, especially, when it was considered appropriate for a man to write to the woman with whom he had spent the night.

The letters were works of art in themselves. Paper, a rather precious commodity in those days, was made in different thicknesses, textures, and colors, each of which came to possess a suggestive meaning of its own. The message or poem was written on it in calligraphy that was studied by its recipient for its nuance of expression. Did it show sensitivity? Maturity? Daring? Clumsiness? In the early stages of an affair this could be valuable information. After the poem was written, the sheet of paper was then folded into a shape that also could suggest the intentions of the message, and perhaps accompanied by a flower or other item relating to its contents.

When these poems were later selected for anthologies, special presentation copies of the collections were sometimes made on the finest decorated papers. These papers were not only dyed in various colors, but also sprinkled with particles of gold and silver foils and enriched by stamped or painted designs. When these poems were copied onto such pages, they became like a final, fluid curtain of text hung before a gorgeous, imaginary space of gold clouds and silver snow.

The colored bands of cloudlike forms behind the writing in this album deliberately suggest the decorated papers found in the finest Heian and Kamakura poetry albums, and although they reflect a much later and relatively simplified stage of the tradition, they still give the sense of writing suspended in space in some unreal but exquisite universe.

Relatively few *waka* have been preserved from the ninth century, when the Japanese poem was limited to private occasions. Ono no Komachi is the only women among the group in this album who was active during that time. Her poems, though small in number, are complex, powerful, and passionate, and set a standard for women's poetry that few were able to match. Nothing is known about her life, although she soon became a subject of legend.

Although the ninth-century emperors after Saga were not as fond of Chinese poetry as he had been, they were not particularly supportive of Japanese poetry either; still, the *waka* gradually reentered public life, late in the century. A very important event in this reemergence was the first known poetry competition.

In the summer of 885, 886, or 887, some friends gathered at the home of Ariwara no Yukihira (818–893) to compete with one another through Japanese poetry. Ten rounds were on the subject of the cuckoo and two on unfulfilled love. The poems were preserved, but not the identities of the poets. Its was undoubtedly a casual amusement, probably modeled after *sumō* matches, like other such court competitions, but it caught the fancy of those who mattered. The second competition was held by an imperial consort, and the third was sponsored by Emperor Uda (867–931; r. 887–897) and held in the palace.

Once they were held in front of the emperor, poetry competitions quickly became more serious undertakings. The fundamental elements were as old as court poetry itself: a given topic or theme, competitive composition, and appropriate public presentation. The formal judgments were new, however, and they resulted in a stress on aesthetic quality.

The sponsor of a poetry competition would generally assign one or more topics for the competition, and the participants would be divided into two equal-sized teams, the Left and the Right. Sometimes there was a separate reciter who read each poem, a scribe who recorded poems and judgments, and a scorekeeper. The competition began with the first poet on the Left team, who was generally the most prestigious participant. After the first poem from each side was read, there was usually some discussion by the participants.

It was not unusual for team members to present arguments supporting their side, and on some occasions these discussions became quite heated. Finally a judgment was made, either by a judge or by consensus of the group. If neither could be declared the winner, a tie was awarded. At the more elaborate competitions, a miniature landscape was constructed for each team, either to receive the poems or to keep score by a visual device, for example, by adding chrysanthemums to the model. At the end of the prescribed number of rounds, the teams with the most wins was declared the victor.

Poetry competitions helped to restore the prestige of Japanese poetry at court, and they produced a supply of publicly available poems. But the great event that fully established the *waka* at the heart of the Japanese cultural tradition and that set the standards for the next five hundred years of composition was the compilation of the *Kokin wakashū*. Emperor Uda's successor, Emperor Daigo (885–930; r. 897–930), ordered the anthology in 904. Although he was quite young, Daigo was very interested in Japanese poetry and court ceremony. The principal compiler was Ki no Tsurayuki (868?–945), who was Director of the Imperial Library.

Tsurayuki, with the help of his team of compilers, not only formed a model for selecting and organizing *waka* that lasted through twenty successors over five hundred years, he also articulated in the anthology's preface a philosophy of poetry and a basic poetics that gave it direction and method. The beginning of the *Kokin wakashū* preface is one of the most famous passages in Japanese literature:

> The Japanese poem takes human emotion as its seed and grows into the myriad leaves of words. Because the affairs and activities of man in society are so numerous, people speak out, entrusting what they feel in their hearts to things seen and heard. When we hear the warbler that sings in the blossoms, or the voice of the frog living in the water, we wonder whether there is any living thing that does not compose poetry. Poetry is that which, without any exercise of force, moves heaven and earth, arouses the emotions of the invisible spirits and gods, harmonizes the relations between men and women, and also soothes the hearts of fierce warriors.

In essence, he claims, poetry is the expression of deep personal feeling, and it is composed by connecting internal feelings to the external events and objects of the world.

The central position accorded to emotion in Japanese poetry is evident in the strong interest in love poems throughout the tradition. Love provided the ideal motivation for poetry because it inspires such intense feelings, and yet it remains complex. Most of the poems in this album are about love, but they combine desire, anger, sadness, frustration, confusion, joy, despair, fear, and hope in often ambiguous mixtures. Although these poets wrote from a strong emotional position (either actual or imagined), their aim was more often to qualify and complicate that feeling than to express it clearly and simply.

Women were more closely associated with love poetry because their ambivalent social situation with regard to men gave them a natural advantage in writing about mixed emotions. Men were in a clear position of power and could determine exactly when and whom they would woo and visit with little risk.[14] Male poets sometimes adopted the persona of a woman in love, though women rarely took the position of a man.

The public, court context in which poetry was appreciated placed limitations on its subject matter and methods. Poets were expected to find new refinements and approaches to a standard repertoire of themes rather than try to extend the scope of experiences in poetry. The vocabulary in *waka* is relatively limited, but the exact nuance of each word was considered extremely important. The poet Fujiwara no Teika wrote:

> The most important thing in poetry is the choice of words. Many of them are either strong or weak. Distinguish between them carefully. Strong words should be joined together with other strong words, and weak words with other weak

ones. In this way, keep thinking and rethinking them, until there are no fat parts and no thin parts and there is no roughness or dissonance. This is extremely important. In other words, on the whole words are neither good nor bad, simply the way they are linked together determines success or failure in poetic language. It is very unattractive to link words of mysterious beauty with words of violent force. Always start with the emotion as the basis, and then select and discard words accordingly. That is what my late father [Fujiwara no Shunzei] told me.[15]

Two fundamental types of *waka* were recognized: those that expressed an emotional condition directly, and those that described a mental state indirectly, usually through reference to some external phenomenon. Although the direct expressive method is usually associated with the poems in the *Man'yōshū* and the second type with the *Kokin wakashū*, both types are present in each of these anthologies and in all later collections. Nonetheless, styles shifted as poets changed the ways in which they preferred to make those connections, or changed the referents. Their strongest expressive weapons were complex grammatical structures and the rich atmosphere of connotations that came to surround the words and themes considered fundamental to the tradition.

The success of the *Kokin wakashū* and the complete acceptance of Japanese poetry in the tenth century as an important public activity of the court were two aspects of a broader movement that replaced or supplemented some Chinese cultural practices with alternatives developed in Japan. But in the time of the *Kokin wakashū*, the influence of Chinese literature remained very strong, and Chinese poetry provided poets of the *waka* with a vast, pretested pool of images that could be used as metaphors for their own feelings, and that gave Japanese poems a head start on the road of increasing complexity of expression. It also provided models for technical developments, such as the manipulation of persona and the use of rhetorical devices. As the tradition matured, poets drew more often on earlier *waka* than on Chinese sources, and by the Kamakura period they also called on important works of prose in Japanese, such as *The Tale of Genji*, to expand their repertoire of allusions.

This process of accumulation and refinement is so different from the attitudes of most Western art and literature that, after the initial exoticism of Japanese poetry passes, the sense of repetition can threaten to become overwhelming. It is important to realize that the aesthetics of Japanese poetry is analogous to the appreciation of calligraphy. Creativity in calligraphy is demonstrated not by the invention of new characters or letters, but by the expression of a new beauty and sensitivity within the limitations of existing parameters. The subtle details matter most, but they are sometimes difficult to grasp in isolation. For that reason the commentaries on the poems in this album attempt to create a context of other poems within which a particular example seeks its own voice.

The Poets

All of the poets in this album were active at the court in Kyoto. One was a princess, Shikishi Naishinnō, and one was an imperial concubine, Saigū no nyōgo. Because of their very high ranks and positions, these two are shown in this album seated on tatami mats behind curtains of state. The only other poet of particularly high position was Daini no sanmi, daughter of Murasaki Shikibu, who owed her rise in the world to the fact that she was wet nurse for an emperor. One poet, Nakatsukasa, was the daughter of a prince and had no known court position. One poet, Michitsuna no haha, was the mother of a prominent political figure and a noted author. The history of one poet, Ono no Komachi, is virtually unknown.

The remaining thirty poets all served as ladies-in-waiting, primarily to emperors or their consorts. Although social conditions changed constantly during the more than three centuries spanned by these poets, it is safe to say that except for Shikishi Naishinnō, Saigū no nyōgo, and (by promotion) Daini no sanmi, all of these poets are part of the middle levels of the aristocracy. Their positions serving the important figures of the court were both sources of pride for their families and heavy responsibilities for the women. For most courtiers, success in life was gained through the skillful managing of relationships with others who were yet closer to the center of prestige and authority.

Except in the very beginning of the Heian period, when Emperors Kammu and Saga ruled as well as reigned, the authority of the emperor was continually under assault by the upper nobility, in particular the main branch of the Fujiwara family. By establishing their daughters as imperial consorts, these aristocrats assured that they would be related to the child who became the next emperor. This was an effective strategy when the new emperor was still a young child. If he became independent-minded later on, he was encouraged to retire in favor of one of his children. Court politics was extraordinarily complicated, as each family at every level was struggling to create relationships of dependence and association that would provide protection and offer new possibilities for advancement.

The imperial harem with its numerous consorts, all of whom were daughters of important aristocrats, became a kind of battleground for influence. The opening section of *The Tale of Genji*, which tells how rival ladies destroy the emperor's favorite, describes the intensity of the competition. These consorts were very young—the aristocracy usually married in their early teens—and an important duty of many of these poetically gifted ladies-in-waiting was to provide literary assistance and expertise to the members of the court. They were key to creating and maintaining an atmosphere of artistic achievement and tradition at court.

Every part of the court had its organizing system of ranks and offices, and the women's quarters was no exception. Each of these ladies occupied a specified position in the hierarchy from which they hoped to advance. Six of these poets, for example, have the title *naishi* (Suō no naishi, Uma no naishi, Ben no naishi, Koshikibu no naishi, Gofukakusa-in no shōshō no naishi, and Gidōsanshi no haha). This indicates that they held positions in the Office of Palace Attendants (*Naishi no tsukasa*), which was one of twelve offices in the women's quarters at the palace. The ladies in this office were responsible for, among other things, daily attendance on the emperor along with petitions, palace etiquette, and meals.

In the mid-Heian period, when women's writing reached its peak, some of these poets, most notably Sei Shōnagon, Michitsuna no haha, and Murasaki Shikibu, left memoirs and diaries that give vivid pictures of their lives, and that have been translated into English.[16]

The illustrations of the poets in this album are imaginary portraits, but they follow in a long tradition of depictions of court ladies. Except for the two important ladies who are shown seated on tatami mats behind screens of state, the poets are shown without any setting other than an occasional writing desk or armrest. This portrait form can be traced back to the first illustrations of Kintō's set of Thirty-six Immortal Poets. The earliest extant examples are sections from a mid-thirteenth-century pair of scrolls called the *Satake bon* ("Satake volumes") because it was once part of the Satake Collection.[17] Alongside each of the poets depicted in these early scrolls is that person's name, a short biography, and a poem. All but five of the poets are men, and they are distinguished to some degree by their clothing, which reflects their ranks and positions through colors and accoutrements.

By contrast, women's court dress did not display such clear signals of rank or position, although they did manifest an important artistic sensibility. The dress consisted of an underrobe; long red trousers whose legs dragged behind; up to twelve layers of fine-quality robes, each slightly different in size so that the range of their colors was visible at the collar in front and at the ends of the huge sleeves; a pleated train; and a jacket. The proper color coordination of these many parts was a sophisticated matter that was not taken lightly. In her diary Murasaki Shikibu spends many pages describing what women wore and how it affected those around them. One incident is especially interesting, because it seems that even Murasaki was not sure where the mistake was made:

> All the women were in their best that day, but two of them showed a want of taste when it came to the color combination at their sleeves. As they brought in the food, they came into full view of the nobles and senior courtiers and were subjected to stares. I later heard that Lady Saishō had been scandalized. But it was not that much of a faux pas, just that the combinations were somewhat uninspiring. Kodayū was wearing a crimson unlined dress with robes of five layers in differing shades of crimson with purple linings. Her jacket was white lined with deep red. Genshikibu seemed to be wearing robes of deep crimson lined with purple and a damask mantle of crimson lined again with purple; perhaps it was because her jacket was not of figured silk, but then that would have been ridiculous.[18]

These robes were a considerable burden to carry around and made it difficult to move about. It is not an accident that women were usually shown seated. The colorful impression of the robes was accented by the women's black hair, which, uncut, extended even as far as the floor when they were standing. The ladies of the court powdered their faces, shaved their eyebrows and repainted them higher on the forehead, and blackened their teeth. The folding wooden fans that they held were used to help shield their faces in public, although they rarely went outside or traveled, except in heavily screened ox-drawn carriages.

In this album these poets of the ancient past have been reimagined by the artist Hosoda Eishi. Eishi, whose name as an artist was Chōbunsai, was the eldest son of a distinguished samurai family, and studied painting under Kanō Eisen-in Michinobu, an official painter to the shogunate. Eishi was himself favored with the sponsorship of the shogun Tokugawa Ieharu, whom he served for three years until 1783, when he asked to be released on the grounds of illness. After setting out on his own he turned to ukiyo-e prints, illustrating books and designing individual prints and series. His style was especially elegant, featuring tall, thin women in graceful poses, and he created a number of prints with literary themes. Because of his family background and his relationship with the shogunate, Eishi considered himself to be on a higher social level than most other printmakers of his time. In 1800 he had the honor of presenting a painting to Empress Gosakuramachi; that same year, he stopped making prints altogether and returned to painting for the remainder of his life.

Eishi designed one other book of poets at the end of his printmaking career: *Yatsushi sanjūrokkasen* (Thirty-six Immortal Poets in Modern Dress), a playful updating of the venerable subject. By contrast, the poets in this album are drawn in a way that faithfully follows the models of the past. In fact, we can compare the portraits in this album to a mid-eighteenth-century painted handscroll of the same subject in the Spencer Collection. The handscroll, called *Nyōbō sanjūrokunin utaawase* (Poetry Match of the Thirty-Six Immortal Poetesses),[19] is closer than the album to earlier traditions of poet painting. Competing poets are shown facing each other with their poems written directly above them. Only five of the poems in the handscroll are also in the album, so it is clear that the two works follow different textual recensions. But the poses of the poets are uncannily similar for all but six of the first eighteen illustrations.

The relationship between the portraits of the poets in the handscroll and those in the album suggests that the tradition of illustration of The Thirty-six Immortal Women Poets may have been somewhat established by 1800. Most illustrated versions of The Thirty-six Immortal Women Poets date from the seventeenth century, when the subject seems to have reached its peak of popularity. Unfortunately, no illustrated versions older than the Edo period have been discovered, so it is difficult to trace the history of this portrait tradition with confidence.[20]

It is not clear why The Thirty-six Immortal Women Poets suddenly became fashionable in the early Edo period. The general circumstances of the time—a revival of interest in court culture and the art patronage of the rising urban class—are only a partial explanation. Perhaps, as in the case of this album, it reflected a new interest in the education of women.

Eishi was not content, however, simply to follow established models, whether from the previous century or earlier, for his portraits. He most radically departs from his ancient models in those cases where he shows the poets standing—for example, in the portraits of Michitsuna no haha, Izumi Shikibu, Ben no naishi, and Shikikenmon-in no Mikushige. In stances inconceivable in classical Japanese painting, these tall women provocatively look over their shoulders like Edo courtesans in ancient dress. But Eishi succeeds most brilliantly in the portrait of Daini no sanmi, whose standing image with her long curve of hair and winglike sleeves is simultaneously poised and energetic.

Eishi has also suited the images comfortably to the album format. In the handscroll tradition, each lady was fully drawn with all parts of her dress visible, but in the album the format has been allowed to crop the images. This enlarges the image of the poet within the frame and creates a sense of dramatic tension that is missing in earlier versions.[21] In addition, Eishi has given new life to the clothing that sometimes threatens to overwhelm these poets. It was a considerable challenge to an artist's graphic skills to make a series of such similar images seem interesting. Eishi cleverly varies the density and harmonies of the textile designs along with the abstracted folds and lines of the robes. And he is most successful when, despite all odds and expectations, he is able to suggest the shape and movement of an individual poet underneath her mass of brilliant clothing.

Perhaps, then, just as we attempt to envision—through Eishi's portraits—the actual histories of the women poets who animate these attractive robes, so, too, do we strive to appreciate their emotions and creative individuality, expressed through words that are themselves so carefully and cleverly embroidered.

1. This story is recorded in *Fukuro sōshi* in Sasaki Nobu-tsuna, ed., *Nihon kagaku taikei* (Tokyo: Kazama shobō, 1964), vol. 2, p. 57.

2. *Sanjūrokkasen* literally means "thirty-six poetic immortals," and is a reference to the Taoist immortals of Chinese mythology, sages who had acquired the secrets of immortality through Taoist practices. In Kintō's time there was a tradition of the *Rokkasen* (literally "six poetic immortals"), a term that describes the six poets who were specifically mentioned and criticized by name in Tsurayuki's preface to the *Kokin wakashū*. As the first important critical statement on poetry, and because of the prominence of the anthology, this preface was enormously influential, and the poets were called sages even though all the criticism is negative. Kintō included thirty-six poets in his selection because the number is six sixes.

3. See *Gunsho ruijū*, vol. 13, pp. 347–49, for the text of this earliest version.

4. MYS 17, 18.

5. Mori Asao, "Sento: Ōmi sento to Miwayama aibetsu-ka," in *Man'yō no kyokō*, ed. Ōkuma Kiichirō (Tokyo: Yūsankaku shuppan, 1977), pp. 38–56.

6. Helen Craig McCullough, trans., *Kokin wakashū* (Stanford: Stanford University Press, 1985), p. 276.

7. The abbreviations are based on the short forms of the anthologies' names, which leave out the word *waka*. Thus *Kokin wakashū* is often called *Kokinshū* and abbreviated KKS. Heian and Kamakura poets often went even further and just called it *Kokin*. The numbers that precede the names of each anthology refer to a chronology of all imperial

anthologies compiled between ca. 905 and 1314. Several of these anthologies are not represented in the album, hence the absence of numbers 3, 6, 9, 12, and 13.

8. Ono no Komachi was in such demand by anthology compilers that a number of forgeries and misattributions were included as her work.

9. Kuroita Katsume et al., eds., *Ruijū kokushi, Kokushi taikei*, rev. and enl. ed. (Tokyo: Yoshikawa kōgunkan, 1979), 2:388.

10. Mezaki Tokue, *Heian ōchō*, Nihon no rekishi bunko, vol. 4 (Tokyo: Kōdansha, 1975), pp. 29–30.

11. See Helen Craig McCullough, *Brocade by Night* (Stanford: Stanford University Press, 1985).

12. Kitayama Shigeo, *"Man'yō no sōzōteki seishin* (Tokyo: Aoki shoten, 1960), pp. 87–88.

13. In the next stage, the late Heian period, it became customary for the man to move into his wife's house. Only in the thirteenth century did women regularly leave their homes to live with their husbands. See Takamure Itsue, *Nihon kon'in shi: ren'ai ron*, Takamure Itsue zenshū, vol. 6 (Tokyo: Rironsha, 1967). See also William H. McCullough, "Japanese Marriage Institutions in the Heian Period," *Harvard Journal of Asiatic Studies* 27 (1967), pp. 103–67.

14. The best guide to the complex relationships between men and women in Heian Japan is *The Tale of Genji*, but, since it is a romantic novel, there are some important differences between the world of the book and the real world of the time. To appreciate these differences, see Haruo Shirane, *The Bridge of Dreams: A Poetics of "The Tale of Genji"* (Stanford: Stanford University Press, 1987).

15. *Meigetsushō*, in *Nihon kagaku taikei*, vol. 3, p. 348.

16. See Selected Readings in this volume for the most important of these.

17. For more on the tradition on paintings of poets as seen in other works in the Spencer Collection, see Miyeko Murase, *Tales of Japan* (New York and Oxford: Oxford University Press, 1986), pp. 56–64 and 70–74.

18. Richard Bowring, trans. *Murasaki Shikibu: Her Diary and Poetic Memoirs* (Princeton: Princeton University Press, 1982), pp. 151–53.

19. For a description and some photographs of this scroll, see Murase, pp. 62–65.

20. Mori Tōru, *Kasen-e hyakunin isshu-e* (Tokyo: Kadokawa shoten, 1972), pp. 31–45.

21. Eishi's skill in fitting the poets into the rectangular album format can best be appreciated by comparing this album with two seventeenth-century printed books of the same subject that are much less visually effective. See Mori Tōru, pp. 41, 43.

Notes for the Commentaries

Ono no Komachi

1. KKS 552.
2. MYS 3738.

Shikishi Naishinnō

1. SKKS 1035.

Ise

1. KKS 780.
2. KKS 982.
3. See *Ise shū* (Wakashi kenkyūkai, ed., *Shikashū taisei*, [Tokyo: Meiji shoin, 1973], vol. 1, p. 217, poem no. 4.). A variant of this poem is KKS 1049, attributed to "the Minister of the Left," who was another of Ise's loves, Fujiwara no Tokihira.

morokoshi no	Even if she hid
yoshino no yama ni	On a Yoshino Mountain
komoru tomo	In far-off China,
okuremu to omou	Though I am not a person
ware naranaku ni	Who would want to stay behind. . .

This variant also allows a range of interpretation since the final *ware naranaku ni* could be either exclamatory ("I certainly am not one who would want to stay behind!") or concessive ("Although I am not one who would want to stay behind. . ."). The recipient could not be sure from the words alone whether the poem pledged or hedged.

Kunaikyō

1. ShokuKKS 88.

Nakatsukasa

1. GSS 847.
2. KKS 205.

Suō no naishi

1. GSIS 765.
2. SKKS 1212.
3. This chain of poems can probably be carried at least one poem farther. A contemporary of Priest Anbō's daughter, Minamoto no Michinari (d. 1019), wrote this poem that was included in the *Goshūi wakashū* (GSIS 950):

itsushika to	Although pointlessly
machishi kainaku	I waited, asking myself,
akikaze ni	"When will it happen?"
soyo to bakari mo	Without even a whisper
ogi no oto senu	The reed grass produced no sound.

4. ShokuKKS 1296.

Saigū no nyōgo

1. She was the daughter of Price Shigeakira, son of Emperor Daigo (885–930; r. 897–930). Her given name was Kishi. She spent nine years of her childhood (936–945) as the priestess (*Saigū*) of Ise Shrine. At the age of nineteen she became an imperial consort (*nyōgo*) to her uncle, Emperor Murakami (926–967; r. 946–967), by whom she bore a daughter.
2. SKKS 1210.
3. KKS 758.
4. MYS 947.

Shunzei no musume

1. SKKS 1136.
2. KKS 747. The circumstances are described in *Ise monogatari*. See Helen McCullough, trans., *Tales of Ise* (Tokyo: University of Tokyo Press, 1968), p. 71.

Ukon

1. GSS 1050. The *Gosen wakashū* version opens with *tou* ("visit") rather than *au* ("meet"), and the fourth measure reads *iso ni ya idete* rather than *iso ni idete ya*, but these variations do not appreciably affect the meaning. The wording here is found in other competitions of The Thirty-six Immortal Women Poets.

Taikenmon-in no Horikawa

1. SZS 916.

Michitsuna no haha

1. See Edward Seidensticker, trans., *The Gossamer Years*. Rev. ed. (Rutland: Charles Tuttle, 1973), p.
2. SKKS 1239. The third measure in the competition text, *toubeki ni*, is *toubeki o* in *Kagerō nikki*, *Shinkokin wakashū*, and other texts. I have assumed that *toubeki o* is correct.

3. Murai Jun, ed., *Kagerō nikki zenhyōkai*, 2 vols. (Yūseidō, 1978), vol. 1, pp. 155–56.

4. The ending *nuru* in *taenuru* and the *ni* of *inikeri* are different forms of the same verb suffix, which is used to indicate that the action of the verb has come to take place at the conclusion of some period of development or expectation. The final *keri* of *inikeri* adds the sense of fresh realization or understanding, even surprise.

5. Other central images: *kage*, which means both the reflection of an image in a mirror or on the surface of water and also the mental image of an absent person; and *katami*, "memento," which is derived from a combination of *kata*, "form, shape," and *mi*, "see."

6. MYS 378.

Gishūmon-in no Tango

1. SKKS 1794. The standard *Shinkokin wakashū* version has *koborenuru* in the third measure, but this difference in the verb ending does not significantly change the meaning.

2. KKS 847.

3. *Koke* was used to describe not just moss and lichen, but also ferns, and I visualize the wind sweeping down from the pines and across the ferns to the poet in her rustic mountain hermitage.

4. Kunaichō shonikubu, ed., *Katsura miya bon sōsho* (Tokyo: Yōtokusha, 1961), vol. 14, p. 290. It is interesting to compare the two poems in this round of the 1204 competition. Both conclude with a two-measure noun phrase describing the wind in the pines, but Gishūmon-in no Tango's choice of words is much more creative. The verb *kayou* ("sweeps back and forth") describes movement from one point to another and back again, and it also suggests a complex interpenetration. Moreover, the final noun phrase skillfully completes the poem's opening, since the wind through the pines is revealed as the sound that the poet hears. By contrast, the last two measures of Tadayoshi's verse are rather ordinary and they do not complete the previous three measures, but lead forward uncertainly. His poem feels incomplete.

Uma no naishi

1. Uma no naishi served Kishi, consort of Emperor Reizei (950–1011; r. 967–969); Kōshi, consort of Emperor En'yū (959–991; r. 969–984); Princess Enshi; and finally, Teishi, consort of Emperor Ichijō (980–1011; r. 986–1011).

2. SKKS 1209.

Kayōmon-in no Echizen

1. SKKS 1140. The *Shinkokin wakashū* version has *hete mo* rather than *futomo*. The meanings are the same, as both are

equivalent forms of the same verb, and the double meaning, "to set up the loom with the warp threads," is not affected either.

2. KKS 703. Anonymous.

3. Notes on early texts of the *Kokin wakashū* claim that this poem was a reply to a poem sent by an emperor to a female court attendant (KKS 702).

Akazome Emon

1. Richard Bowring, trans., *Murasaki Shikibu: Her Diary and Poetic Memoirs* (Princeton: Princeton University Press, 1982), p. 131.

2. The English translation and commentary is McCullough, W., and McCullough, H., *A Tale of Flowering Fortunes* (Stanford: Stanford University Press, 1980).

3. SZS 565. The last line of the *Senzai wakashū* version is *ochishi namida ni*, which here means the same as *otsuru namida ni*.

Nijō-in no Sanuki

1. SZS 878.

2. *Mumyōshō* by Kamo no Chōmei (1155–1216). See *Kagaku taikei*, vol. 3, pp. 298–99.

3. KKS 710.

Izumi Shikibu

1. Bowring, p. 131.

2. Edwin Cranston, trans., *The Izumi Shikibu Diary* (Cambridge: Harvard University Press, 1969).

3. KYS 660.

4. This poem was highly regarded by two great poets: Fujiwara no Shunzei, who included it in *Koraifūteishō*, the treatise and anthology he prepared for Princess Shikishi (see Round 1) in 1197; and Fujiwara no Teika, his son, who selected it for his *Kindai shūka*, an anthology of model poems prepared for the instruction of shogun Minamoto Sanetomo in 1209.

Kojijū

1. SKKS 1664.

Kodai no Kimi

1. Before that time Kodai no Kimi served Empress Kōshi (947–979), consort of Emperor En'yū.

2. SKKS 1042.

3. *Zoku kokka taikan*, poem no. 16798, p. 242.

Gotoba-in no shimotsuke

1. ShokuGSS 374.

Murasaki Shikibu

1. Bowring, p. 135.
2. SKKS 820.

Ben no naishi

1. ShokuGSS 238. The anthology version has *kusaba no ue*, "tops of the blades of grass," in place of *kusaba no kage*, "undersides of the blades of grass." This makes better sense, and all of the other published versions of the *Competition of The Thirty-six Immortal Women Poets* that contain this poem also use *kusaba no ue*, so we can safely presume that *kage* is a copyist's error unique to this recension.
2. This assumes that we accept *kusaba no ue to* as the proper wording, rather than *kusaba no kage to*.

Koshikibu no naishi

1. GSIS 1002.
2. *Fukuro sōshi*, written in 1159. In Sasaki Nobutsuna, ed., *Nihon kagaku taikei* 2 (Tokyo: Kazama shobō, 1964), pp. 63–64.

Gofukakusa-in no shōshō no naishi

1. ShokuKKS 1321. This poem is directly based on a poem by the male poet Fujiwara no Okikaze (active ca. 900) in the *Kokin wakashū* (KKS 814):

uramite mo	Though I feel bitter
nakite mo iwamu	And even though I may cry
kata zo naki	There is nothing to say.
kagami ni miyuru	Without another's reflection
kage narazu shite	Visible in my mirror

Okikaze is adopting the persona of a woman whose lover has stopped visiting. As long as he is absent there is no point in trying to put her feelings into words. Gofukakusa-in no shōshō no naishi's poem knowingly adopts the same situation, but replaces the mirror with the moon and, through an interesting twist, claims that no later pain could equal the cold indifference of the moon on that night, presumably the one on which he left her.
2. For this reason the poem is cited frequently in poetry treatises. See, for example, *Toshiyori zuinō*, in *Nihon Kagaku taikei*, vol.1, p. 129.
3. SKKS 591.

Ise no tayū

1. GSIS 585. The *Goshūi wakashū* version differs in two minor points: *iki mo kaeranu*, "he will not go and return," in place of *mata mo kaeranu*, "he will not return again," and *hito zo koishiki*, "how I long for him," in place of *hito*

zo kanashiki, "how sorrowful I feel when I think of him." Both known recensions of her personal anthology, *Ise no tayū shū*, contain the final line *hito zo kanashiki* for this poem. And the variant *mata mo kaeranu* is standard in other versions of the competition.
2. KKS 146, by an anonymous poet.

Inpumon-in no tayū

1. SKKS 1228.

Sei Shōnagon

1. Ivan Morris, trans., *The Pillow Book of Sei Shōnagon*, 2 vols. (London: Oxford University Press, 1967).
2. GYS 1252.
3. KKS 472.

Tsuchimikado-in no kozaishō

1. According to her alternate name, Shōmeimon-in no kozaishō, she earlier served Emperor Tsuchimikado's mother, Zaishi (1171–1257).
2. ShokuKKS 77. The *Shokukokin wakashū* version has *tsukete* rather than *tsurete* in the second measure.
3. Tamagami Takuya, ed., *Genji monogatari hyōshaku*, 14 vols., vol. 2, pp. 336–37.

Daini no sanmi

1. Daini no sanmi married Fujiwara no Kanetaka, bore him a daughter in 1025, and became wet nurse to Emperor Goreizei. Later she married Takashina no Nariakira and had a son by him in 1038. Her name derives from the fact that she was promoted to Junior Third Rank (*sanmi*) in 1045, and her husband Nariakira held the government position of *Daini*. In her earlier years she was called Echigo no ben.
2. SZS 908 in most editions, SZS 910 in some others.
3. SZS 557, sent to Fujiwara no Nagaie (1005–1064). He replied:

tare mo mina	Though it is not true
tomarubeki ni wa	That every single person
aranedomo	Can keep on living,
okururu hodo wa	When the time comes to part
nao zo kanashiki	What sorrow I feel nonetheless.

Hachijō-in Takakura

1. SKKS 1270.
2. See, for example, MYS 3650.
3. KKS 775 (anonymous).

4. MYS 983. See also MYS 985, 1372, 2010, 2043, 2051, 2223, and 3611 for the alternate names *tsukuyomiotoko* and *tsukihito'otoko*, both of which mean essentially "moon-man."

5. Tamagami Takuya, ed., *Genji monogatari hyōshaku* (Tokyo, Kadokawa shoten, 1969), vol. 11, p. 136.

6. GSS 685.

Gidōsanshi no haha

1. GSIS 907.

Gosaga-in Chūnagon no tenji

1. ShokuGSS 963.

Ichinomiya Kii

1. SKKS 646.

2. It helps to go back to the beginning. One of the earliest winter plover poems was written by Ki no Tsurayuki (868?–945), the principal compiler of the *Kokin wakashū*, and a key figure in the court poetry tradition.

omoikane	Restless with longing,
imogari yukeba	I go out to meet my love.

fuyu no yo no	On this winter night
kawakaze samumi	How cold is the river wind.
chidori naku nari	I hear the plovers crying.

The poem was included in the *Shūi wakashū*, compiled around 1006. SIS 224.

Shikikenmon-in no Mikushige

1. ShokuGSS 1184.

2. KKS 952.

3. There is also a tradition of reading *iwao no naka* as "inside the crag," as in a cave.

4. A precursor is found in SIS 652.

5. ShokuGSS 647. See also ShokuGSS 660.

Sagami

1. GSIS 695.

2. *Sagami shū*, poem no. 121, in *Shikashū taisei*, vol. 2, p. 254.

Sōhekimon-in no shōshō

1. ShokuKKS 1305.

Selected Readings

Bowring, Richard. *Murasaki Shikibu: Her Diary and Poetic Memoirs*. Princeton: Princeton University Press, 1982.

Brower, Robert H., and Miner, Earl. *Japanese Court Poetry*. Stanford: Stanford University Press, 1961.

———. *Fujiwara Teika's Superior Poems of Our Time: A Thirteenth-Century Poetic Treatise and Sequence*. Tokyo: University of Tokyo Press, 1967.

Cranston, Edwin A. "The Dark Path: Images of Longing in Japanese Love Poetry," *Harvard Journal of Asiatic Studies*, vol. 35, 1975, pp. 60–100.

———, trans. *The Izumi Shikibu Diary*. Cambridge: Harvard University Press, 1969.

Forrer, Matthi. *Hokusai*. New York: Rizzoli, 1988.

Hirshfield, Jane, with Mariko Aratani. *The Ink Dark Moon: Love Poems by Ono no Komachi and Izumi Shikibu*. New York: Charles Scribner's Sons, 1986.

McCullough, Helen Craig. *Brocade by Night: "Kokin Wakashū" and the Court Style in Japanese Classical Poetry*. Stanford: Stanford University Press, 1985.

———, trans. *Kokin Wakashū: The First Imperial Anthology of Japanese Poetry*. Stanford: Stanford University Press, 1985.

———, trans. *Tales of Ise: Lyrical Episodes from Tenth-Century Japan*. Tokyo: Tokyo University Press, 1968.

McCullough, William H., and Helen Craig McCullough, trans. *A Tale of Flowering Fortunes: Annals of Japanese Aristocratic Life in the Heian Period*. 2 vols. Stanford: Stanford University Press, 1980.

Miller, Roy Andrew, *The Japanese Language*. Chicago: University of Chicago Press, 1967.

Morris, Ivan, trans. *As I Crossed a Bridge of Dreams*. New York: Harper and Row, 1971.

———, trans. *The Pillow Book of Sei Shōnagon*. 2 vols. Oxford: Oxford University Press, 1967.

Morse, Peter. *Hokusai: One Hundred Poets*. New York: George Braziller, Inc., 1989.

Rodd, Laurel Rasplica, and Mary Catherine Henkenius, trans. *Kokinshū: A Collection of Poems Ancient and Modern*. Princeton: Princeton University Press, 1984.

Seidensticker, Edward G., trans. *The Gossamer Years*. Rev. ed. Rutland: Charles Tuttle, 1973.

———. *The Tale of Genji*. 2 vols. New York: Alfred Knopf, 1976.

Shirane, Haruo. *The Bridge of Dreams: A Poetics of "The Tale of Genji."* Stanford: Stanford University Press, 1987.

Tahara, Mildred, trans. *Tales of Yamato: A Tenth-Century Poem-Tale*. Honolulu: University Press of Hawaii, 1980.

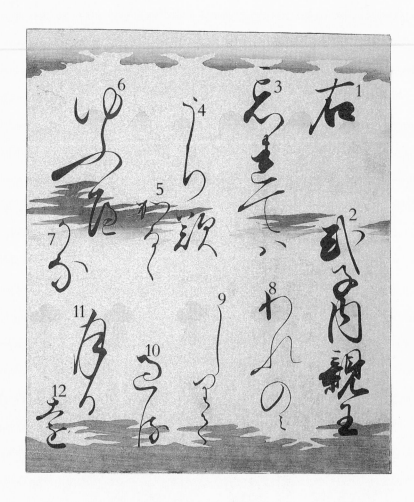

Calligraphy

This note is a guide to reading a poem in this volume, for example the one by Shikishi Naishinnō reproduced on this page as well as on p. 183. As in the modern language, the text is written in a mixture of *kanji* (Chinese characters) and *kana* (syllabary). To make the difference clear, I have transliterated the words represented by *kanji* in capital letters. In 1800, the syllabary was larger than it is today (and larger still in the Heian and Kamakura periods) so that a single sound could be represented by more than one different but equivalent *kana*. We read here, of course, in the oriental tradition of top to bottom, and right to left.

1. MIGI ("Right")	5. ka ru ru	9. shi ri te
2. SHIKI SHI NAI SHIN NŌ	6. yu fu be	10. SUGU ru
3. WASU re te wa	7. ka na	11. TSUKI HI
4. u chi NAGE	8. wa re no mi	12. o

General Notes

Biographies of the poets are based primarily on the entries in Ariyoshi Tamotsu, ed., *Waka bungaku jiten* (Tokyo: Ōfūsha, 1982). All dates are approximate.

The romanization of the poetry texts follows the standard transliteration for modern pronunciation except in the case of the sentence-final-form of verbs such as *tou* ("visit"), where I felt that the spelling *tō* would have needlessly obscured the grammar. For the purposes of meter, a syllable consists of a vowel, or a consonant and a vowel. Long vowels, such as *ū* or *ō*, count as two syllables.

Vowels should be pronounced as in Italian, and consonants as in English, all with relatively even stress, in order to approach the correct modern pronunciation. The pronunciation of these poems by their authors would have been quite different, however, since the language changed significantly over the five-hundred-year span represented by these verses as well as in the seven hundred years since the last was written.

The numbering of poems is in accordance with the texts in Matsushita Daizaburō, ed., *Kokka taikan* and *Zoku kokka taikan*, reprints (Tokyo: Kadokawa shoten, 1958), except for poems from the *Senzai wakashū*, which are misnumbered in this edition of *Kokka taikan*. *Senzai wakashū* numbers follow Yamagishi Tokuhei, ed., *Hachidaishū zenchū*, 3 vols. (Tokyo: Yūseidō, 1960). The third volume of this set is my source for the count of each poet's works in imperial anthologies.

To view and to read the second part of this volume, please turn to page 192. The pages in this section are organized in the Far Eastern tradition of bookmaking, that is, from right to left, or from 'back to front' for the Western reader.

Translations of the Afterwords and Colophon

Afterwords

In the past, between the Engi era [901–922] and the Kenji era [1275–1277], there were many thousands of skilled poets. Among them, in particular, there were thirty-six talented women who were exceptional ladies of the court and who were especially creative with language. Later generations of admirers hung their portraits in their houses and carved their writings in plaques over their doors. And it is not surprising that it is impossible to add anything to their lovely words and beautiful pictures.

Recently someone urged me to have the young girls in my school write out these poems, so that, together with illustrations by Mr. Hosoi, they could be printed, bound, and distributed to people with similar interests. For a long time I had had something of the same intention, but to proceed hastily and to pursue readers ignorantly would arouse the criticism of the wise. So I declined and set it aside for a while to wait for another opportunity. Again and again he kept talking to me about it, and eventually I agreed.

I feel that this enterprise is a very modest one, too small to merit either praise or criticism. All I want is to bring back to life the accomplishments of these talented poets so that these children can make speedier progress. It should also be more than a little useful to those who come after my students.

Mr. Tachibana, Tekigaiko,[1] agrees with me completely. I do not want to ignore anyone's suggestions.

Finally, I direct the woodblock carvers and artist to set to work.

> *Edo, Hasegawa street*
> *Hanagata Yoshiakira*
> *Ninth year of Kansei [1797], mid-winter.*

1. Although it seems from context that the three characters that form Tekigaiko are used to refer to Tachibana no Chikage, this is not one of his standard pseudonyms.

The poetry competition in this volume was written by the young girls studying under our teacher Hanagata Yoshiakira in their own hands. The calligraphy was completed earlier and the illustrations that followed have now, this winter, also been finished. Since a publisher kept on asking for this book, our teacher recently decided to consider the merits of publication. Our wish is to encourage the further efforts of these girls and to participate in the elegant poetic tradition.

> *Written by Hanagata Hide.*

This competition of The Thirty-six Immortal Women Poets was recorded here by the young girls who study with me under the master. It should demonstrate how fine our master is and how superior the teaching that he offers us. Although I am not particularly talented, the master told me to write a line at the end of this book and I have done so. Do not think badly of me.

Written by Kawamura Yoshimichi, age fourteen.[1]

1. Yoshimichi is a male name, and we can safely presume, I think, that he was the leading boy student at the Hanagata shōdo.

Colophon[1]

Poems recorded in Edo by thirty-six young girls of various families studying at the Hanagata shōdo. Approved by their master, Hanagata Yoshiakira.

Illustrations drawn in Edo by Hosoi Chōbunsai.

Woodblock carvers: Yamaguchi Matsugorō and Yamaguchi Kiyozō.

Soon to be published:
Thirty-six Poems and Portraits in Color Prints
One volume.
Calligraphy by boys from various families who are students of Master Hanagata.

Previously published:
Thirty-six Poems by the Master of Monkey Mountain Illustrated with Color Prints
One volume.
Illustrations by Katsukawa Shunshō

Calligraphy completed: Kansei 10 [1798]
Published: Kansei 13 [1801], Spring

Founder: Nishimuraya Denbei

Edo main store
Bakurō-chō ni-chōme
Eijudō
Nishimuraya Yohachi

1. As the colophon is missing from the Spencer Collection edition of the album, I have used, for the text of this page, the photograph of the British Museum edition published in Klaus J. Brandt, *Hosoda Eishi 1756–1829: Der Japanische Maler und Holzschnittmeister und seine Schuler* (Stuttgart: K. J. Brandt, 1977), illus. 138, no. 400.

きえずとふくらましより
ふんてはば波めをこたかまれし
ぞうゑんたまひそ

いつ村美路
空みて
記

此女房三十六人談合ひまして

ともに師べ候よくくふらしくく

めりける野のいとをうつ

とをたりたくくく(ゑれ

がしことをもそめり川

ぬししおのれをさえけくふ

あきてはりうくれま一と

女華勸業而ニ風流ゑ一端也

花形ひてや識

Hanagata Hide (2)

右歌谷一帖者花谷義離先生
門下契所各自書也今在之
冬書既成畫而續牽業須日
肖書韓来頓結而不舍則為
先生以古聽鑵擇是非新別

不花容清書...

寛政九丁巳仲冬　花形義艶

東都長谷川街

Hanagata Yoshiakira (1/b)

自謂此草也揚羽聿筆尖
夫不足以察於末功之道
亦北有獨於世既作後輩
亦既既然知善所以為畫
以有言無復不可以美可
不以若楷其又無善之事乃

Hanagata Yoshiakira (1/a)

近奉遣詣治云古以弱苑
以春豊魚數十石而就
中三十六下日買棹匹之
寺一女新得也
莫之去寺軍去尸棹之
章操師亂隋無復渡於園

18ʀ / *Sōhekimon-in no shōshō*

Sōhekimon-in no shōshō was an attendant to Sonshi, also known as Sōhekimon-in, consort of Emperor Gohorikawa. She was the daughter of the important poet Fujiwara no Nobuzane, participated in a poetry competition in 1243, and was still alive in 1276. Sixty-one of her poems were included in imperial anthologies. This poem was selected for the Love section of the *Shokukokin wakashū* with the simple headnote "From a group of love poems."[1]

It makes an excellent contrast to Sagami's poem. Both are about desire but are set at opposite ends of the conventional experience of love. Sagami's interest is carnal and optimistic, and her language is visual and complex. Shōshō's concern is abstract and pessimistic, and her words are ironic and proselike. It is as if these final two poems express the two opposite poles both of the emotions surrounding love and of the use of language in poetry.

Sōhekimon-in no shōsho cleverly incorporates religious ideas. The phrase that she uses for "die," *mi o kae*, literally means "to change bodies" and describes the passage from one cycle of existence to the next in the continual round of reincarnation. The life that she has obtained this time, that is, the life of a human being, is "in accordance with my wishes" (*kokoro no mama*) because this is the life to which all other forms of beings aspire. It is the one in which it is possible to hear the Buddha's teaching and to move toward achieving the enlightenment that ends the painful cycle of birth and death. In other words, she may be suggesting that after so many rounds of birth and death, she finally has achieved a human form; now will she just throw it away because of a failure of love? The opportunity of this life is precisely to gain freedom from such desires.

But that religious reading emphasizes the importance of the original sense of *mi o kae*. An alternative interpretation could place more weight on *kokoro no mama*, which literally means "in accordance with the heart." A life of this kind is one that proceeds naturally and without obstacles. Now that she has met the difficulty of frustrated desire for the first time, will she give up and move on to the next life? Not likely.

How appropriate that this competition should end with a poem that addresses the whole experience of love but that does not have a clear position on it. Despite the strong conventions of the literary tradition, poetry could still be composed, because at the same time that the poetry of the past gave depth and poignancy to one's private experiences, it also recognized the possibility of a personal voice, even if it had to be hidden, like the bodies of the ladies, under confusing layers of beautiful coverings.

sore o dani
kokoro no mama no
inochi tote
yasuku mo koi ni
mi o ya kaetemu

I had thought that
This life at least would be one
That went as I wished.
Why then must I give it up
So easily, because of love?

18ʟ / *Sagami*

Sagami is thought to have been born around the turn of the eleventh century. She married Ōe no Kinyori, governor of Sagami Province, and went there with him in 1020. When he returned to Kyoto for reassignment they separated, and she had an affair with Fujiwara no Sadayori (995–1045). Sagami became an attendant to Princess Shūshi, and was very active in court poetry circles until around 1060. She was very highly regarded for her love poetry, as were Izumi Shikibu and Ono no Komachi before her, and one hundred eight of her poems are in imperial anthologies.

This poem was selected for the Love section of the *Goshūi wakashū* and appears with this headnote: "At a time when she was secretly in love, her best friends—did they recognize her desire?—said, 'Why do you seem so moody?' and in her heart she responded with this poem."[1]

The uninhibited enthusiasm of this poem stands out against the careful poses of most of the other poems in this competition. But the headnote restores a conventional posture to some extent by denying that she actually sent it or even wrote it down. The compiler of the *Goshūi wakashū*, about a generation after Sagami's death, probably found it in her collected works, where it appears with this headnote: "At a time when her love was secret, there was an embarrassing incident, and, although she did not resolve [to send it], nonetheless she wrote this poem."[2]

As was true of the love poetry of Komachi and Izumi Shikibu, the passion in this verse is symbolically communicated, here, through two double meanings that relate the act of tying a cord to their union: *morotomo ni . . . tokubeki*, "we will relax together" and "we will untie together"; *au koto no kata . . .*, "difficult to meet with one another" and "hard to fasten." The climactic *shitahimo*, "under-sash," is made even more suggestive by *yowa*, "night," and by *katamusubi naru*, which describes a casual way of fastening in which one end of the cord is wrapped loosely around the other. Expecting him, she hasn't even tied a proper knot.

It is interesting to note that the three women who most clearly represent the tradition of passionate love poetry, Ono no Komachi, Izumi Shikibu, and Sagami, are positioned precisely at the beginning, middle, and end of the Left team, as if they constituted the fundamental structure around which the rest of women's poetry is built. And is it, I wonder, a coincidence that the first and last poems of the Left team are the only love poems on that side that are not complaints?

morotomo ni
itsuka tokubeki
au koto no
katamusubi naru
yowa no shitahimo

When can we relax
Together, for one another
That so hard to join
But so easily loosened
Knot that fastens my night clothes?

18R / *Sōhekimon-in no shōshō*

古　藻鹽

世をいとふこゝろの
このもとは
やとく花さへ

君よやかさし草

四日市　九世院女十五歳書

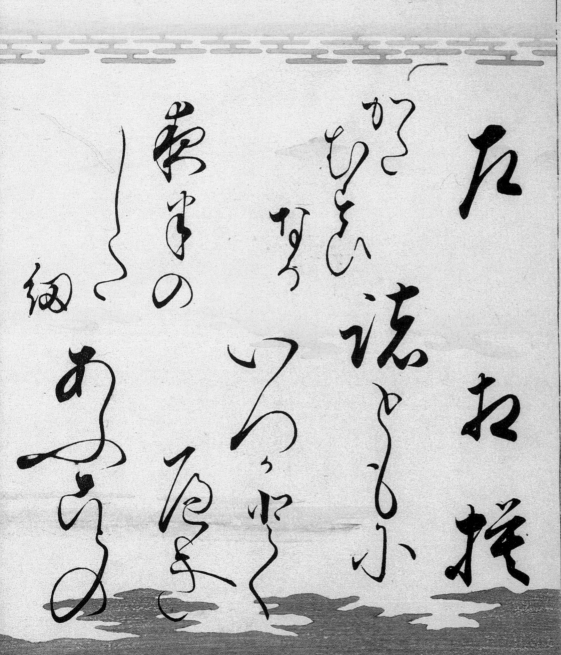

摂州同明町　山口瀧　四十壱章

17ʀ / *Shikikenmon-in no Mikushige*

Shikikenmon-in no Mikushige's dates are unknown, but we know that she was active during the middle of the thirteenth century. The daughter of Fujiwara no Michimitsu, she served Shikikenmon-in until the latter's death in 1251. She then attended Nashi (1209–1283), a grand-daughter of Emperor Takakura who was granted the title Ankamon-in by Emperor Gohorikawa (1212–1234, r. 1221–1232) in 1224. The poet was accordingly also known as Ankamon-in no sanjō. She lived at least as late as 1263. Fifty of her poems are in imperial anthologies. This poem was included in the Miscellaneous section of the *Shokugosen wakashū*, without a headnote.[1]

The point of the poem, that there is no escape from sorrow in life, no matter where you live, echoes Buddhist teaching, but also specifically restates a poem in the *Kokin wakashū*:[2]

ika naramu	In what kind of place
iwao no naka ni	Amid the mountain crags
sumaba ka wa	Could I make a home
yo no ukikoto no	Where the world's miseries
kikoekozaramu	Would not be audible?

This poem placed the phrase *iwao no naka*, "amid the mountain crags," firmly in the poetic vocabulary as the symbol of the ultimate escape.[3]

Mikushige's creative contribution is to involve the phrase *mi o saranu*, which first achieves acceptance into the poetic vocabulary with this poem.[4] Literally it reads "does not avoid itself" and is used to mean "inescapable," "unavoidable," "intrinsic." It can have religious overtones, as in this verse by the Buddhist priest Prince Kakujo (1250–1336), in which it refers to the innate enlightened mind:[5]

mi o saranu	Before the moon of
kokoro no tsuki ni	My inescapable mind
kumo harete	The clouds are clearing.
itsu wa makoto no	When will I be able to see
kage mo mirubeki	The shining light of truth?

The word *ukiyo*, literally "world of misery" or "world of suffering," is also a Buddhist concept. And of course the remote mountaintop is a favorite location for serious religious practitioners. All of these points gives Mikushige's poem a decidedly religious flavor.

In the Edo period the ebullient society of the pleasure quarters was also called *ukiyo*, but the word was written with the characters that mean "floating world" rather than "sorrowful world." This sporting parody of the ancient and somber Buddhist term expressed the irreverent atmosphere so well that it came to be used to describe this important new subculture and the art (*ukiyo-e*) that it inspired.

mi o saranu

onaji ukiyo to

omowazu wa

iwao no naka mo

tazune mitemashi

If I did not expect

The same, inescapable

World of suffering

I would try to find a place

Amid the mountain crags.

17ʟ / *Ichinomiya Kii*

Ichinomiya Kii served Princess Yūshi, the eldest daughter (*ichinomiya*) of Emperor Gosuzaku (1009–1045; r. 1036–1045), and hence was known as Ichinomiya Kii, or, more commonly, Yūshi Naishinnōke no Kii. Kii is known to have participated in poetry competitions sponsored by Yūshi and others between 1061 and 1113, but the details of her history are unclear. Twenty-nine of her poems are in imperial anthologies.

As in Ukon's poem in Round 5, this poem uses part of a place-name (*Fukiage no hama*) as a pivot word: "In the bay winds that are whipping up, Whipping-up Beach has its sand plovers." The syntax is further complicated by the fact that "In the bay winds" connects with "rising waves," while "sand plovers" links with "I hear their cries." The result is a sophisticated grammatical cross-weaving of birds and waves.

The poem appeared in the Winter section of the *Shinkokin wakashū*[1] with a headnote indicating that it was one of the one hundred poems that Kii included in an offering to Emperor Horikawa. This event is thought to have taken place in 1105 or 1106. Fourteen poets each composed a set of one hundred verses (one each on one hundred assigned topics) in three major sections, Seasons, Love, and Miscellaneous, following the structural pattern of imperial anthologies. The project was carefully orchestrated by two poets close to the emperor, and was the beginning of the influential practice of composing poem series of one hundred verses. This poem was Kii's response to the topic of plovers (*chidori*), one of fifteen topics in the Winter section.

The *chidori* are generic small birds that fly in flocks, often on the shore (*chidori* literally means "thousand birds"). These little birds gradually appeared in winter poems as poets made use of the anomaly of the activity of these apparently defenseless birds in the wind and cold. Kii's poem is an effortful attempt to work just one more plover poem out of the standard images, by using complex wordplay and by making poetry tradition supersede reality. Since the plovers are often linked in poetry with waves, she presumes that since she can hear the birds in the middle of the night, the waves must be rising, and the waves rise, in turn, because they are at a shore whose name implies a rising wind. If this seems more like chess than poetry, it is probably because the poetic possibilities for plovers had been nearly exhausted by Kii's time.[2]

urakaze ni
Fukiage no hama no
hamachidori
nami tachikurashi
yowa ni naku nari

In the bay winds
That are Whipping-up Beach
Has its sand plovers.
Rising waves must be coming in.
I hear their cries in the night.

17ʀ / *Shikikenmon-in no Mikushige*

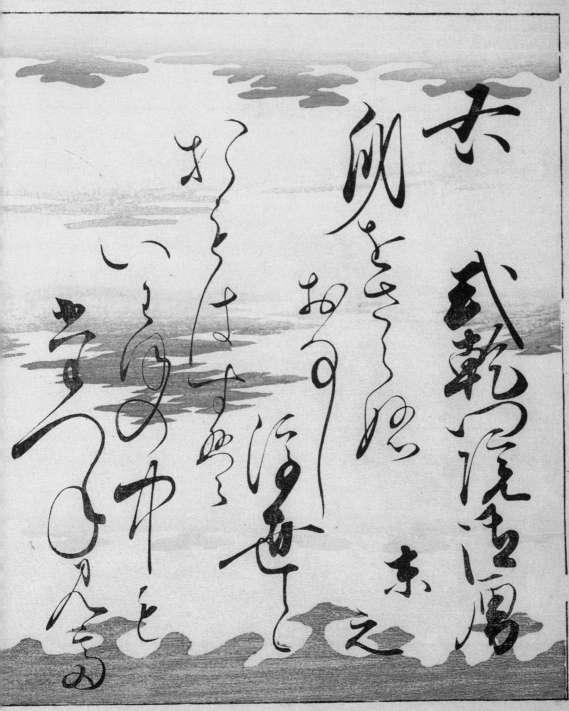

豊名所
山田や
々三 十三
枚ま

17L / *Ichinomiya Kii*

両国柳橋枚原七四十二寸まて

左

一夜泡伊

みやら
くく
浦風よ
まもち
かしり

あまみ
いそれ

菊小
みそれ
それ
こまの

16R / *Gosaga-in Chūnagon no tenji*

The poet here identified as Gosaga-in Chūnagon no tenji is somewhat better known as Tenji Shinshi no Ason or Chūnagon no tenji. Her given name is Shinshi and she was the daughter of Hamuro no Mitsutoshi (1203–1276), a leading poet of the time who is usually referred to by his religious name, Shinkan. As one of her names suggests, she was once in the service of Emperor Gosaga. Thirty-three of her poems are in imperial anthologies. This poem was selected for the Love section of the *Shokugosen wakashū*, where it appears without a headnote.[1]

The first part of the poem is more prose than poetry, but the second introduces some ambiguity. *Kawaru narai* could mean either "changing habits" or "habit of changing." *Yo* could mean "life," "society," or "our relationship." This allows the final statement to be philosophical ("a life where change is habitual"), social-historical ("a society of changing habits"), or personal ("our relationship where your change of heart is habitual"). Even the first part of the poem could be either abstract (if we read *hito* as referring to men in general) or personal (if we take it to mean "you"). The appropriateness of emphasizing one of these readings over another depends mostly on context.

Japanese poets were extremely sensitive to the role of the reader and the context in determining meaning. In *The Tale of Genji*, in which the circumstances surrounding the composition and exchange of poems are frequently described, considerable attention is given to the implications of paper type and color, calligraphy style, and accompanying objects or gifts. In the imperial anthologies, where poems were culled from private exchanges, public events, literary exercises, and past anthologies and collections, a new context and order were established by separating the poems into topical sections (Seasons, Love, Laments, and so on) and then organizing them within each section. In the Love sections, for example, poems are positioned according to the stage of love they are chosen to represent, from longing and first glimpses at the beginning of the section to lonely despair at the end.

The first poem in this round, by Gidōsanshi no haha, was placed at the beginning of the Love section of the *Goshūi wakashū*, and in that setting reflects the early, playful, flirtatious phase of a relationship, while Shinshi's poem, near the end of the Love section of the *Shokugosen wakashū*, is situated to represent a detached bitterness. She is so far beyond blame that she is willing to presume the good intentions of liars. The experience of love, as is generally true within this classical poetic tradition, is ultimately a lesson in the unreliability of life.

itsuwari to
omowade hito mo
chigirikemu
kawaru narai no
yo koso tsurakere

Men, without thinking
That they are in fact lies,
Have made promises.
What hurts is this life of mine
Where change is habitual.

16L / *Gidōsanshi no haha*

Gidōsanshi no haha ("mother of the deputy minister") is the name most commonly used for the poet Takashina Kishi, whom this text calls Kō no naishi ("attendant from the Takashina family"). Her birth date is unknown, but she died in 996. She was the wife of the leading politician Fujiwara no Michitaka (953–995) and the mother of Korechika (973–1010) (the deputy minister), Takaie (979–1044), and Teishi (977–1000). Teishi was installed as imperial consort by her powerful father, and included Sei Shōnagon in her entourage (see Round 14). At one time Kishi was also an attendant to Emperor En'yū. Gidōsanshi no haha was in fact more significant historically as a wife and mother than as a poet. Five of her poems are included in imperial anthologies, and these are the only works by her that survive.

This poem appears in the Miscellaneous section of the *Goshūi wakashū* with this headnote: "At a time when the Regent [Fujiwara no Michitaka] was just beginning to visit her, on the morning after failing to come to her he sent her a message saying, 'Last night it was so hard for me to get through the night, etc.,' and she composed this poem in reply."[1]

This is exactly the sort of sharp, sarcastic response that Heian courtiers seemed to love. Michitaka pretends that he spent the long night waiting for dawn and thinking of her, and Kishi replies by accusing him of being with another woman. There were sometimes legitimate reasons that prevented men from visiting their ladies, including a complex system of directional taboos that sometimes made it impossible to travel to the necessary part of town. But, in fact, the need to visit other women was usually the most pressing reason in this small, polygamous society for not turning up at night as expected.

Of all the nights not to have a visitor, a night in autumn was considered particularly difficult to get through because it was felt to be so long. Autumn in the lunar calendar used in ancient Japan corresponds approximately to the months of August, September, and October in our calendar, so the relative length of the night was more psychological than actual.

Again, an error crept into the text of this album. The twelve-year-old calligrapher forgot to include the last line of the poem, which is why this text page looks so much less crowded than the others. This is a very unusual mistake in a poetry manuscript, since all poems have the same length.

hitori nuru

hito ya shiruran

aki no yo o

nagashi to tare ka

(kimi ni tsugetsuru)

Would it not take one

Who slept alone to know it?

Who could have told you

That the nights in autumn

Are indeed extremely long?

16R / *Gosaga-in Chūnagon no tenji*

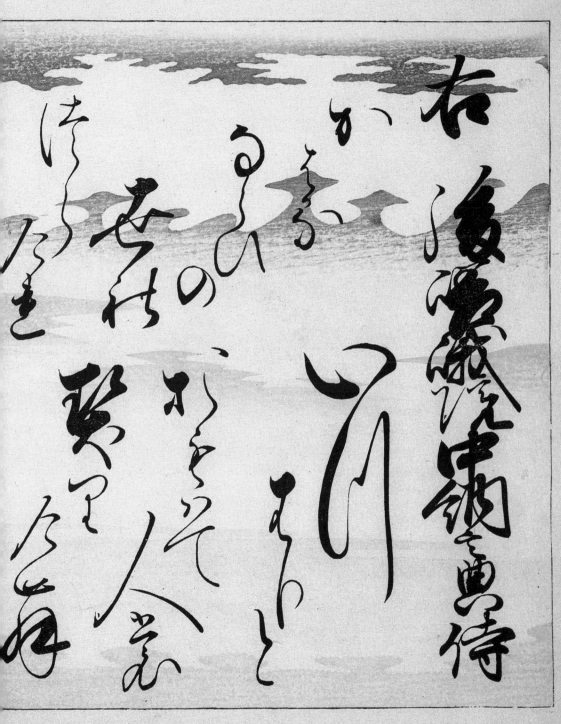

右濱嵐にたえぬゆゑ侍

かもしける

ひとの安居の

山川

ほけゝのせに

もる月そて人こそ

けゝろうみ

大仏みるを鈴の丁
松井常七四郎書

16L / *Gidōsanshi no haha*

左 高内侍

袖をゆるか
　さ
　み
　つ
　る
　ん
わきの露を
　と
　ば
　か
り
　み
　よ

大川通松山方四十二番画

15R / *Hachijō-in Takakura*

Hachijō-in Takakura was around sixty years of age in 1237, but otherwise her dates are unknown. She served Princess Shōshi (also known as Hachijō-in), daughter of Emperor Toba. Forty-three of her poems were selected for imperial anthologies. This poem was included in the Love section of the *Shinkokin wakashū*, without any headnote.[1]

By this point in the poetic tradition, to lie sleepless at night, staring unhappily at the moon while thinking of an absent love, had become a characteristic pose of the classical poet. In early poetry the moon was eagerly awaited; it facilitated the man's visit and was so beautiful.[2] But as the loss of love became more interesting to poets over the centuries, the night of opportunity became more often a night of lonely pain, as in this poem in the *Kokin wakashū*:[3]

tsukiyo ni wa	On this moonlit night
konu hito mataru	I wait for one who does not come.
kakikumori	I want clouds to form
ame mo furinamu	And the rain to fall as well.
wabitsutsu mo nemu	As I languish, I will sleep.

Hachijō-in Takakura's poem obviously echoes this one, but it also recalls a more obscure tradition, found in the eighth-century *Man'yōshū*, in which the moon is referred to as a small, adorable man rowing his boat across the night sky, as in this poem by the female poet Sakanoue no iratsume:[4]

yama no ha no	How fine it will be
sasaraeotoko	To see your light cross the straits
ama no hara	Of heaven's expanse,
to wataru hikari	Oh tiny and lovely man
miraku shi yoshi mo	On the crest of the mountain!

In the five-hundred-year march from the joyous moon of Sakanoue no iratsume to the depressing moon of Hachijō-in Takakura, the extreme position was that it was unhealthy to look at it at all. In *The Tale of Genji* Prince Niou tells Nakanokimi, "Don't look at the moon when you are alone. You'll lose consciousness and it is very painful."[5] An anonymous poem in the *Gosen wakashū* was written "because there was someone who claimed that 'it is said to be forbidden to admire the moon.'"[6]

hitorine no	I lie alone and
wabishiki mama ni	As long as I stay awake
okiitsutsu	In my forlorn state
tsuki o aware to	There is no way to avoid
imi zo kanetsuru	Admiring this lovely moon.

kumore kashi
nagamuru kara ni
kanashiki wa
tsuki ni oboyuru
hito no omokage

Cover it with clouds!
As soon as I gaze on it
I feel such sadness,
Imagining in the moon
The face of the one I love.

15L / *Daini no sanmi*

Daini no sanmi, whose given name was Kenshi, was the daughter of Murasaki Shikibu. She was born in 999, and was still alive in 1078.[1] Thirty-seven of her poems are in imperial anthologies. This poem was selected for the Love section of the *Senzai wakashū* with the headnote "Sent to a man with whom she had relations, but who had not visited in a long while."[2]

We are brought again to the end of a relationship in this verse. The manner of expression stands out because of the strong formal parallelism and the abstract character of the language. Part one and part two of the poem each contain in the same order the past forms of contrasting verbs (*utagaishi*, "doubted" = *chigirishi*, "pledged") modifying nouns (*inochi*, "span of life," "life" = *naka*, "relationship") that are the subjects of opposite verbs (*ari*, "to live," "to exist" = *tae*, "to die," "to end"). The two parts are hinged by the verb suffix *nagara*, which indicates that the first action is still taking place simultaneous with the second action, and the poem is brought to a close with a set of terminal endings: *nu* (indicating that the end has come after a period of time has passed), *beki* (emphasizing the speaker's assurance), and *kana* (indicating that the poet is emotionally touched by this situation). The only word I have not accounted for in this description is *bakari*, which here means "only," stressing that just one of the pair, namely life, goes on.

The other three poems by Daini no sanmi that were included in the *Senzai wakashū* are similarly sophisticated but somehow impersonal, even when they are responses to actual circumstances. The following poem, for example, she sent to a courtier who was in seclusion following the death of his wife:[3]

kanashisa o	Comfort yourself
katsu wa omoi mo	With the fact that it conquers
nagusameyo	Sorrow just as well.
tare mo tsui ni wa	In the end which one of us
tomarubeki ka wa	Can hope to keep on living.

Eishi's imaginary portrait of Daini no sanmi is a spectacular composition. The face and hand of the beautiful lady suggest that she is thoughtful, even hesitant, while the sleeves of her robe seem to explode diagonally outward with mysterious energy. Even the many-layered corners of the robes at her feet lift up as if they were alive. And over it all flows her long, loosely tied black hair like a mountain stream.

utagaishi
inochi bakari wa
arinagara
chigirishi naka no
taenubeki kana

While this span of life
In which I had placed no faith
Continues to endure,
The union that you had pledged
Has come, it seems, to an end.

15R / *Hachijō-in Takakura*

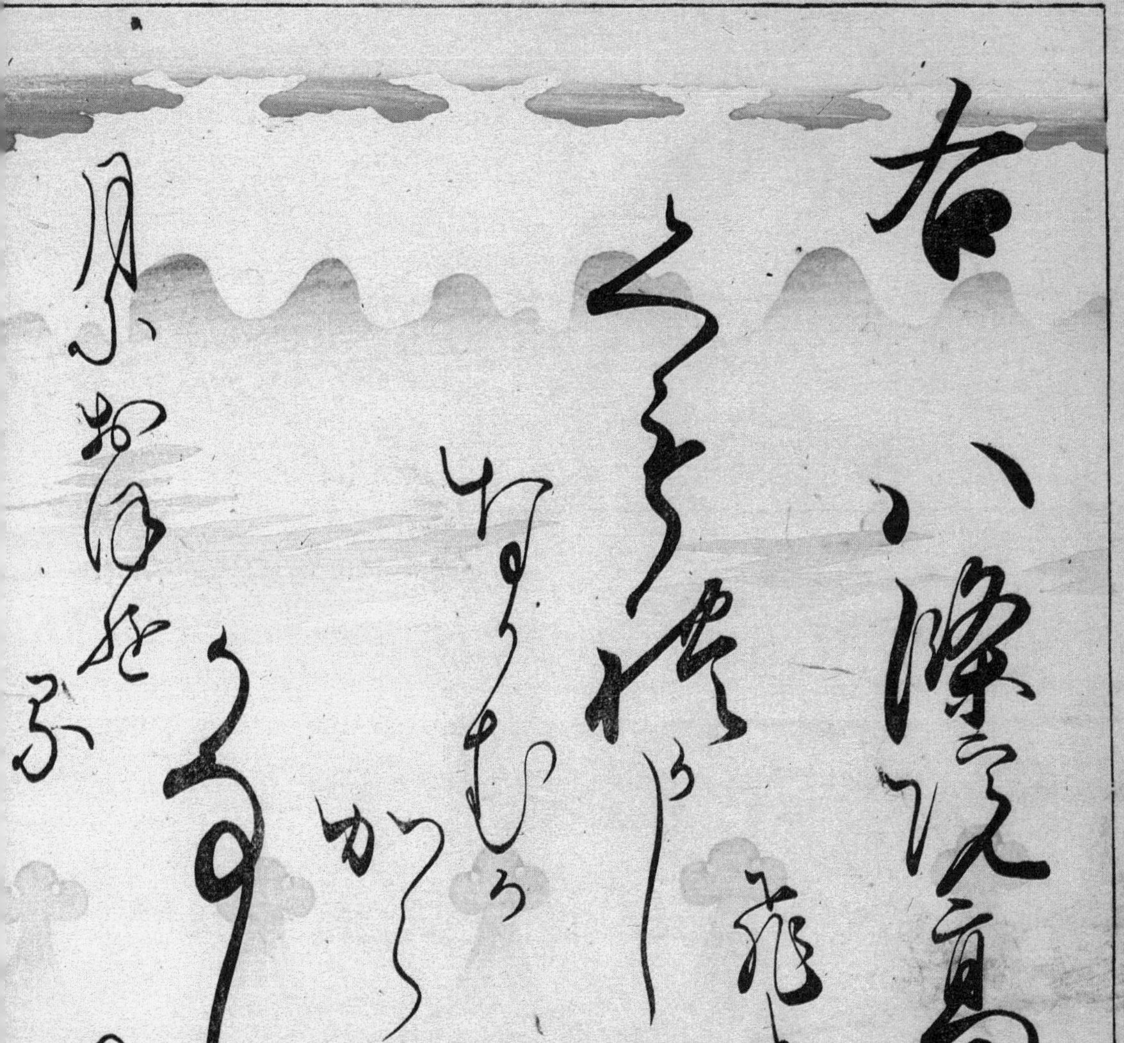

右　ハ瀬入道寂蓮

くもゐにも

すみなれし花よの

かくろ小

里

月のおもてを

ふく

小倉百人一首
橋かくの三の卅十五毎書

15L / *Daini no sanmi*

右　大武三伝

あつかくし命

あつるる　琴て

田所町　寺田なるめ十六事

14ʀ / *Tsuchimikado-in no kozaishō*

Tsuchimikado-in no kozaishō was the daughter of the important poet Fujiwara no Ietaka (1158–1237). Six of her brothers and one sister are also known as poets. As her name indicates, she served Emperor Tsuchimikado (1195–1231; r. 1198–1210), son of Emperor Gotoba and himself a poet.[1] Thirty-seven of her poems are in imperial anthologies. This poem was selected for the *Shokukokin wakashū*, Spring section, with the headnote "Among fifteen verses composed at the home of the former chancellor [Minamoto no Michimitsu]."[2]

The poem is directly based on a verse in *The Tale of Genji*:

fukaki yo no	Those who understand
aware o shiru mo	The beauty of deepest night
iru tsuki no	Have, I think, a bond
oboroke naranu	As extraordinary
chigiri to zo omou	As the setting moon is bright.

This is a poem that Prince Genji spontaneously composes as part of his seduction of Oborozukiyo, a court attendant. He is responding to her remark, "There is nothing like a night with a veiled moon." This is not the casual comment that it seems, but a sophisticated reference to a verse by a late ninth-century poet and scholar of Chinese, Ōe no Chisato:

teri mo sezu	Nothing can compare
kumori mo hatenu	To a night of veiled moon
haru no yo no	On a night in spring
oborozukiyo ni	When the light does not shine forth
shiku mono zo naki	But clouding is not complete.

The language of Chisato's poem is bookish and sounds like a literal translation from the Chinese; in fact, it is thought that he is in turn responding to a line in Chinese poetry about a "veiled moon, not bright, not dark."[3]

Chains of references like this are not unusual in Heian literature. Artistic aristocrats memorized thousands of poems and were able to call them into service as needed. The night with a veiled moon was interesting to these poets because it represents an intermediate, ambiguous state. When the lady drops this line to Genji, she is not only commenting on the natural scene, she is also implying that her own feelings at the moment are uncertain. Just at the moment that the moon sinks below the scattered clouds and shines brightly, Genji recognizes an opportunity. He skillfully applies the two meanings of *oboroke naranu* ("not veiled," "extraordinary") to suggest that, because they both appreciate such aesthetic subtleties as a veiled moon (and the poetic references they generated), they must share some sort of link from a previous life that predestines their love. Finally, Tsuchimikado-in no kozaishō evokes the romantic mood of *The Tale of Genji* delicately and effortlessly.

haru wa nao
kasumu ni tsurete
fukaki yo no
aware o misuru
tsuki no kage kana

Along with the mist
That still rises in this spring
Oh, the light of the moon
Making visible to us
The beauty of deepest night.

14L / *Sei Shōnagon*

Sei Shōnagon (966?–1010–?), a contemporary of Murasaki Shikibu, is best known as the author of *Makura no sōshi*, an entertaining collection of observations and anecdotes that is one of the great works of Heian literature.[1] She married Tachibana no Norimitsu (965–1028–?) around the year 981 and bore a son, Norinaga, but the marriage did not work out, and around 993 she entered court in the service of Teishi, consort of Emperor Ichijō. Teishi's fortunes declined after her powerful father, Fujiwara no Michikane (961–995), died, and her rival, Shōshi, was installed as an imperial consort. Teishi died in 1000 while giving birth, and Sei Shōnagon left court. Her later history is obscure.

Sei Shōnagon's father, Kiyohara no Motosuke (908–990), was a prominent poet, and Sei Shōnagon, like Murasaki Shikibu, was very well educated in both Japanese and Chinese literature. Unfortunately, relatively few of her poems have survived. Sixteen of them are included in imperial anthologies. This poem appeared in the *Gyokuyō wakashū*, in the beginning of the Love section, with the headnote "Sent to someone."[2]

Using *matsu*, which is both the verb "to wait" and the noun "pine," as a pivot word ("I am left to pine. Pinetree Island...."), the poem skillfully integrates two familiar poetic concepts: the breeze that links separated lovers, and the lonely fisherwoman. Under the influence of Chinese poetry, the wind was often spoken of as a messenger, as in this verse from the *Kokin wakashū*:[3]

shiranami no	Even for the ship
ato naki kata ni	That left without a trace
yuku fune mo	Over the white waves
kaze zo tayori no	The wind is a messenger,
shirube narikeru	A guide to lead the way.

The author, Fujiwara no Kachion, a minor poet of the late ninth century, compares himself to a ship. Wherever duty has taken him, it has made it impossible for him to meet his beloved. But the same wind that connects the ship with the land brings memories of her, and will lead him back.

Sei Shōnagon's vessel is a tiny, helpless fishing boat; together they wait for some word from her new beloved, some hint of a breeze. The imagery is reinforced by two double meanings: *matsu*, "I wait," also is part of *Matsushima*, "Pinetree island," and *yosete hisashiki* means both "(the boat) slowly draws near (Pinetree Island)" and "(I) slowly draw closer (to you)." The waiting, then, refers both to Sei Shōnagon's wait for a letter and the fisherwoman's wait for a breeze. Without the letter/breeze, there will be little progress.

tayori aru

kaze mo ya fuku to

Matsushima ni

yosete hisashiki

ama no hashibune

"Bearing some message,

Will the breeze blow?" I am left

To Pine-tree Island

So slowly drawing closer—

The fisherwoman's small boat.

14ʀ / *Tsuchimikado-in no kozaishō*

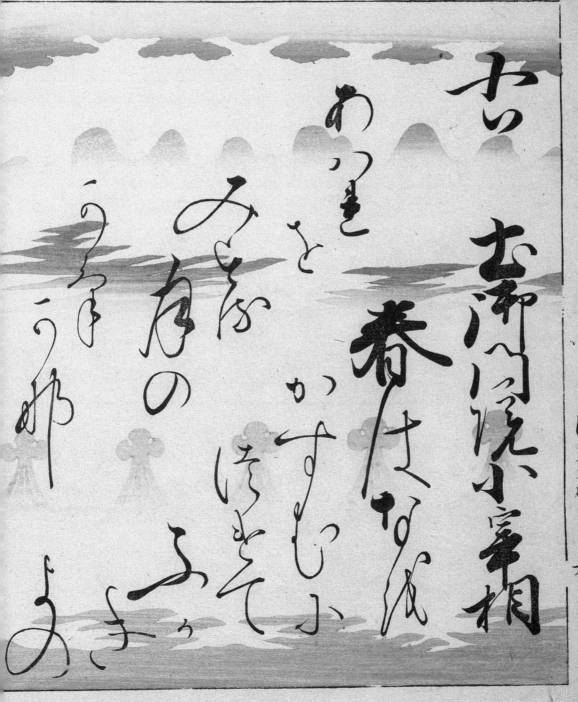

古 左衛門院小宰相

わ里
を
かすみ小
みとな
けほきそて
有の
月の
ふこ
く志て
ふ
み郎
よ

春はな流

深川大ろ町
水田
み兄如丁二歳

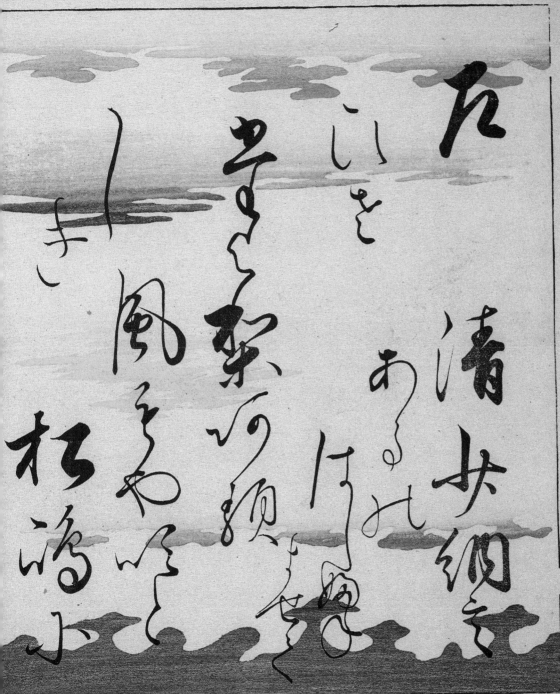

月　清少納言

こしを
あらし

まつ風の頃

ふく風をや峰

まつ松風

南新板　四季画巻　五十二

13R / *Inpumon-in no tayū*

Inpumon-in no tayū was already in service to Princess Kōshi (1147–1214; also known as Inpumon-in), consort of Emperor Goshirakawa, around the year 1156, when she was probably in her mid-twenties. She was active in court poetry circles and became a nun in 1192 when Inpumon-in took vows. She probably died near the end of the century. Sixty-five of her poems are found in imperial anthologies.

This poem was included in the *Shinkokin wakashū* in the Love section, without a headnote.[1] It takes us to the limits of depressive thought, but with some ambiguity. Traditionally there have been two valid interpretations of the opening line: "why do you reject me" or "why do I reject life," depending on whether the reader feels that the poem is addressed to a man or to the poet herself. I am reading the poem as a final attempt to regain the sympathy of an estranged lover. The speaker is too upset to bother with sophisticated language, lyrical allusions, or subtlety of any kind. It is broken into short sentences, and the third measure in particular, *sa nomi ya wa*, conveys the effect of short, shallow breaths reflecting her distress. She is simultaneously angry and desperate, and while the result is effective because it seems so sincere, it is closer to prose than poetry.

The calligraphy of this poem is in the scattered writing style. The poem begins with the more thickly brushed line at the center of the page, continuing diagonally down to the left, and then the calligrapher places the third measure in the two small lines in the lower right and the final measure in the two small lines at the upper right, with the very final syllable floating alone in the upper left. In contrast, the style of presentation for Ise no tayū's poem is conservatively regular, but also shows regard for the formal structure of the verse. It is divided into four upper lines and four lower lines, with a break between them exactly where the row of mushroomlike decorative motif divides the page. The upper four lines exactly contain the first three measures of the poem, while the lower part contains the final two measures. The teachers of the young calligraphers obviously hoped that this book would demonstrate their students' grasp of the many different styles in which a poem could be presented on a page. Although these arrangements were once spontaneous, by the time of this text they had become classified and formalized.

While considerable effort was given here to displaying the variant divisions and positions of a poem on a page, the background decorations under the calligraphy and the style of writing itself are fairly uniform. In the Heian and Kamakura periods, when these poems were first written, this was not the case. An individual at that time was expected to write with a personal style, and the imaginative designs and colors selected for the writing paper were no less a reflection of one's distinctive taste, skill, and character.

nani ka itou
yo mo nagaraeji
sa nomi ya wa
uki ni taetaru
inochi narubeki

Why abandon me?
I can not live any longer.
How could I survive
While enduring misery
As terrible as this?

13ʟ / *Ise no tayū*

Ise no tayū was a contemporary of Murasaki Shikibu and went to court in service to Empress Shōshi around the same time that Murasaki did, in the early eleventh century. She had three daughters whose poems were included in imperial anthologies. Ise no tayū herself had a long career as a poet, extending from her first recognition in 1008 at least until 1060. Fifty-one of her poems are in imperial anthologies.

This round contains the second major error in this edition of the competition. According to this text Ise no tayū is identified in the upper-right-hand corner above her name as a poet on the Right team and Inpumon-in no tayū is noted as a poet of the Left team. But Ise no tayū, like all the other members of the Left team, was an earlier poet, while Inpumon-in no tayū, as is proper for the Right team, is a later poet. Once again it is impossible to know whether the mistake originated with this text or was copied from the source, but no other published version of the competition contains these two major errors: the wrong lines for Gofukakusa-in no shōshō no naishi's poem (see Round 12) and the mislabeling of the poets in Round 13. At the very least we can say that they were probably committed by someone relatively unfamiliar with the subject matter. The portraits were drawn to conform to the team designations in the text, so that since we have reversed their order here to correct the text, the two poets in Round 13 now look at one another over their shoulders, rather than looking away from one another, as was intended by the print artist.

The poem was included in the *Goshūi wakashū*, in the Laments section, with the headnote "Composed the year after Narinobu died, when she was carrying out the final observances."[1]

Ise no tayū uses the idea of the anniversary and the related concepts of the cycle of time, parting, and return to emphasize her sense of loss. The poem is beautifully constructed, with *mata mo kaeranu* ("will not return") referring at first to the date and then, unexpectedly, also to her husband (*hito*). Only at that moment in the last line is the real subject of the poem revealed, and it concludes with a sudden cry of distress.

There is an echo here of a poem from over a hundred years earlier:[2]

hototogisu	Oh cuckoo,
naku koe kikeba	When I hear your voice crying
wakarenishi	What longing I feel
furusato sae zo	Even for that old village
koishikarikeru	Where we were forced to part.

Here too the recurrence of a seasonal event is implicitly contrasted to the irreversibility of the loss of a lover.

wakarenishi

sono hi bakari wa

megurikite

mata mo kaeranu

hito zo kanashiki

That very date

On which we were forced to part

Has come around once more

But will not return again

Nor will he—how sorrowful!

13R / *Inpumon-in no tayū*

左　殷富門院大輔

のらうき
ことおもひ
ならく
光

名町稲荷丹
女十三枚書

13ʟ / *Ise no tayū*

右　伊勢古補

別きても　まこも
そのいも　ゆめ
からや兒　人を恋
くましく　しゝ

小伊せ益町　松井　ふるめ十一帖本

12R / *Gofukakusa-in no shōshō no naishi*

Gofukakusa-in no shōshō no naishi was a poet of the mid-thirteenth century. She was the daughter of the respected poet and painter Fujiwara no Nobuzane and died not long before he did. As her name indicates, she served Emperor Gofukakusa. Her sisters, Ben no naishi and Sōhekimon-in no shōshō, were also poets. All three sisters are represented in this competition (in Rounds 11, 12, and 18). Forty-four of her poems are included in imperial anthologies.

The poem as it is recorded in this album is

uramite mo / nakite mo nani o / kakotamashi / momiji fukiorosu / yamaoroshi no kaze

At some point in the transmission of the text, a copyist made a big mistake by combining the first three measures of Gofukakusa-in no shōshō no naishi's poem with the last two measures of a poem by Minamoto no Saneakira (910–970). The former appears in the *Shokukokin wakashū* in the Love section, with this headnote: "Composed on the subject of 'resentment in love, using moon imagery,' for a poetry competition of ten verses on the thirteenth night of the Ninth Month of the year Kenchō 3 (1251)."[1] We present it here, on the opposite page, in romanized Japanese and translated into English.

Saneakira's poem was very famous, for it contains thirty-four syllables instead of the usual thirty-one, yet was recognized as an extremely fine poem and thus a valid exception.[2] It also appears in major anthologies, including the *Shinkokin wakashū*[3] and Fujiwara no Teika's personal selection, the *Kindai shūka*. The mistake could only have been made by someone rather unfamiliar with classical poetry, since the final two lines were so well known and the poem as written here does not make good sense. We need not blame this error on the twelve-year-old calligrapher, who, as in all of these poems, was probably just copying a model provided by her teachers.

Saneakira's poem:

honobono to	Faintly, faintly
ariake no tsuki no	In the moonlight from the
tsukikage ni	Moon lingering at dawn
momiji fukiorosu	The autumn leaves are blown down.
yamaoroshi no kaze	The wind sweeping down from the mountains.

uramite mo
nakite mo nani o
kakotamashi
(mishi yo no tsuki no
tsurasa narade wa)

Though I feel bitter
And even though I may cry
How can I complain?
Without being as indifferent
As the moon I saw that night

12ʟ / *Koshikibu no naishi*

Koshikibu no naishi (ca. 999–1025) was the daughter of Izumi Shikibu (see Round 9) and, like her mother, was in service to Empress Shōshi. She had a son, Jōen (1016–1074)—who grew up to be a priest and a poet—by the powerful Fujiwara no Norimichi (997–1076), but she was loved by numerous other courtiers; she died soon after giving birth to her second son, Yorihito, by the captain of the palace guard. Eight of her poems are in imperial anthologies. This poem is included in the *Goshūi wakashū*, in the Miscellaneous section,[1] with this head-note: "After Fujiwara no Norimichi had been ill for some days and was recovering, he asked why she had not come to visit him, and she composed this poem."

Koshikibu no naishi reminds Norimichi in her poem that as a woman, and a person far below his exalted rank, it would have been impossible for her to visit him during his illness.

A more detailed and compelling description of the circumstances surrounding this poem was recorded by the poet Fujiwara no Kiyosuke (1104–1177):[2]

> At a time when Fujiwara no Norimichi loved Koshikibu no naishi he fell ill and did not visit her for a long time. After he recovered he went to Shōshi's residence, but Koshikibu no naishi was working in the room where the food stands are stored and he didn't see her until he was leaving. As he was passing her on his way out he said, "I nearly died. Why didn't you visit me?" and kept walking. But she stopped him and replied [with this poem]. He was very deeply moved, and embracing her, he took her to her chambers and made love to her.

Kiyosuke uses this story to demonstrate the value of improvisation. He says: "There are so many stories just like this one. If she had waited several days to reply, it would have been quite different."

It is extraordinary to think that a poem this skillful could be composed spontaneously at an awkward moment. It is not a pastiche of familiar phrases, but it does include a standard double meaning: *ikite* means both "living" and "going," and is commonly found in poems that use *shinu*, "to die."

shinu bakari

nageki ni koso wa

nagekishika

ikite toubeki

mi ni shi araneba

I would have died—

So great was the grief with which

I grieved for you.

Since I am not someone

Who could go and visit you

12R / Gofukakusa-in no shōshō no naishi

右　わが瀬内侍

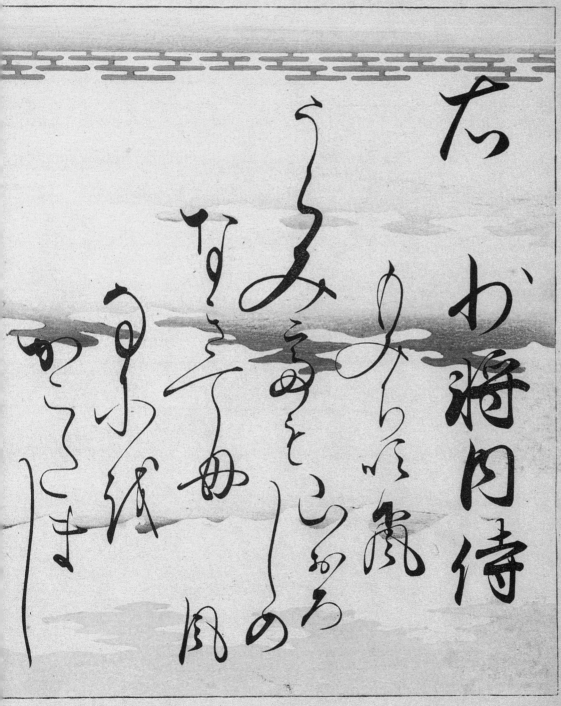

うらみわびほさぬ袖だにあるものをこひにくちなむ名こそをしけれ

小倉百人一首
完　相模七十二首よ

12L / *Koshikibu no naishi*

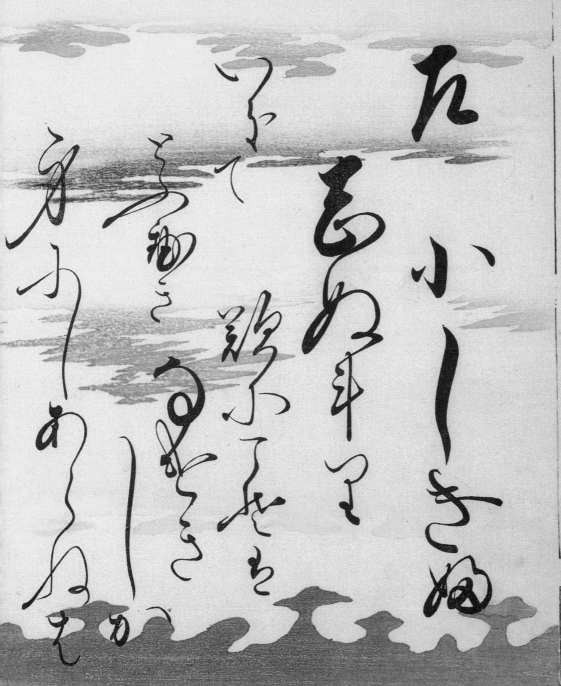

11R / *Ben no naishi*

Ben no naishi served Emperor Gofukakusa (1243–1304; r. 1246–1259) from the time he was crown prince through his abdication. She left court in 1259 and took Buddhist vows in 1265, after the death of her sister, Gofukakusa-in no shōshō no naishi (see Round 12), and just before the death of her father, Fujiwara no Nobuzane (1177–1265). She lived her last years in seclusion in the country. Forty-seven of her poems are included in imperial anthologies. This poem appears in the *Shokugosen wakashū*[1] in the Autumn section, with this headnote: "Composed during a ten-poem poetry competition on the thirteenth night of the Ninth Month, on the subject of early-autumn dew."

The convention of wet sleeves refers as usual to sadness. The poet knows that autumn has arrived not simply because her sleeves are wet as if dew had settled on them, but because she is depressed and has been weeping. Autumn in poetry is the season of sadness. By the late thirteenth century, after four hundred years of refining and elaborating a rather small set of metaphors and conventional images, it had become increasingly difficult for poets to find a compelling voice. This poem was successful primarily because it smoothly joined familiar images and wordings in an appropriate solution to the challenge of "early-autumn dew."

The practice of poetry composition at this level required a thorough knowledge of the canon, particularly the imperial anthologies. Every single measure in this poem had appeared separately at least once in poems in the major anthologies that preceded it.[2] Its only unusual feature, ironically, is the copyist's error in this version, in which *kage,* "underside," has been substituted for the correct *ue,* "top."

In her imaginary portrait, Ben no naishi stands and looks over her shoulder in a commanding stance so typical of the courtesans in the ukiyo-e print tradition that it seems slightly odd she is wearing the long red trousers and multilayered robes of court dress. Her body faces a more classic depiction of Murasaki Shikibu on the previous page, but each is too demure to look directly at her imaginary competitor.

The two poems make an interesting pair because both find the power of speech in old poetic conventions, and both take the familiar voice of a woman in sorrow. We have moved in the competition from expressions of resentment in direct exchange with men to an abstract level of contemplation that is a dialogue with poetry itself.

oku tsuyu wa

kusaba no kage to

omoishi ni

sode sae nurete

aki wa kinikeri

Though I had thought that
Dew formed on the undersides
Of blades of grass,
Even my sleeves are wet—
Autumn has truly arrived.

11ʟ / *Murasaki Shikibu*

Murasaki Shikibu, as author of *The Tale of Genji* (*Genji monogatari*), is Japan's greatest literary figure. She was born probably between 973 and 975, daughter of Fujiwara no Tametoki (ca. 945–ca. 1020), who served in the Ministry of Ceremonial (*Shikibu*). In 998 she married Fujiwara no Nobutaka (950–1001?), an older man with other wives, and she had a daughter, Kenshi, in 999. (Kenshi, better known as Daini no sanmi, appears in Round 15 of this competition.) She started writing *The Tale of Genji* around 1002 and entered court service as an attendant to the eighteen-year-old Empress Shōshi around 1006. Because of her skills as a writer and her knowledge of literature (her father had been a scholar and poet), she was expected to tutor Shōshi and advise her on cultural matters. She was probably called Murasaki after the name of the heroine in *The Tale of Genji*. She was withdrawn and introspective. In her diary she says of herself,

> No one liked her. They all said she was pretentious, awkward, difficult to approach, prickly, too fond of her tales, haughty, prone to versifying, disdainful, cantankerous, and scornful. But when you meet her, she is strangely meek, a completely different kind of person altogether![1]

Among the great poets serving Shōshi, such as Akazome Emon and Izumi Shikibu, Murasaki Shikibu's only close friend seems to have been Ise no tayū (see Round 13). The date of her death is unknown, but some theories maintain that she died in 1014. Fifty-nine of her poems are included in imperial anthologies.

This poem was included in the Laments section of the *Shinkokin wakashū*[2] with the headnote "During a period when she was lamenting how brief life is, she saw paintings of famous places in Mutsu (the far northeast of the country), and wrote this poem." This places the poem in the period of mourning following the death of her husband in 1001. Salt-cauldron Bay (*Shiogama no ura*), the subject of one of the pictures she views, was made famous in poetry as a remote, unhappy place where the sky is filled with smoke from the fires under kettles of brine and from burning seaweed on the beach. Murasaki links this image of smoke to her husband's cremation. Wordplay in the poem is limited to *na zo mutsu* ("its name is Mutsu") in *na zo mutsumashiki* ("its name brings memories").

mishi hito no
keburi to narishi
yūbe yori
na zo mutsumashiki
Shiogama no ura

Since that evening
When the man that I had known
Became no more than smoke,
How its name brings memories—
The Bay of Salt-cauldrons

11R / Ben no naishi

た□□日ゆ

よくゐ（？）て
その□みし（？）け□て
□□□□り
神さぬ□□て秋の
□□□□て

竹のあり今村まつ女十一歳

11L / *Murasaki Shikibu*

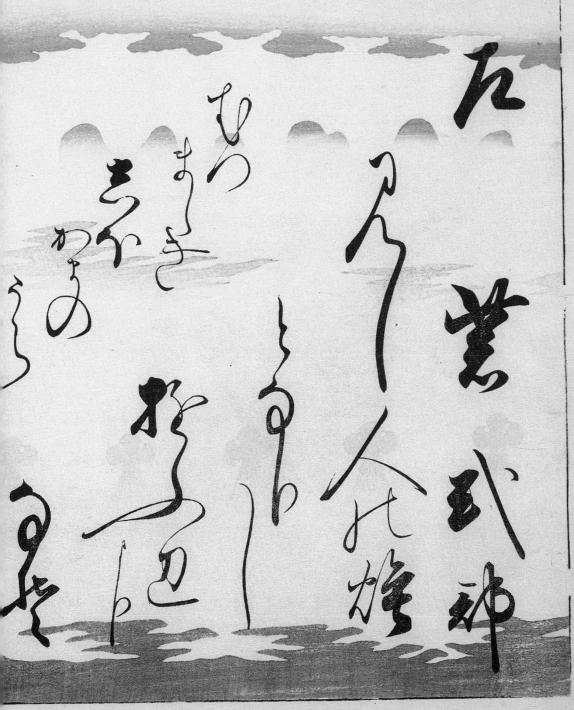

10R / *Gotoba-in no Shimotsuke*

Gotoba-in no Shimotsuke, as her name indicates, served Emperor Gotoba. Around 1204 she married Minamoto no Ienaga and participated in poetry competitions at least as late as 1251. She is sometimes called Shinano. Twenty-five of her poems are included in imperial anthologies.

This poem is included in the Autumn section of the *Shokugosen wakashū*, compiled in 1251 by Fujiwara no Tameie (1198–1275) on the order of Retired Emperor Gosaga (1220–1272; r. 1242–1246).[1] Its headnote reads: "Composed on the subject of crickets when a hundred-poem set was being offered."

This poem is an exercise of courtly wit. The structure is inverted, and the last two measures refer back to the first measure ("Paying attention / . . . To the fitful sleep of the old, / Complaining noisily / Do not cry so intensely / Oh autumn crickets.") Only two words have double meanings: *naki* ("to cry") describes both human weeping and cricket chirping, and *kakotogamashiki*, "complaining," contains *kotogamashiki*, "noisy." But all the other words, except "autumn crickets" and "To the fitful sleep of the old," apply to both settings—to the noisy, complaining crickets that chirp so loudly without caring about the old woman, and to the old woman who complains that the crickets keep waking her up and who tries to keep from crying about her life. The interplay is skillful and alludes to a poetic tradition that links the chirping of autumn crickets through the night with the poet's sad and sleepless state. The poem's main creative feature within this history is the introduction of old age as a cause of the speaker's troubles.

Gotoba-in no Shimotsuke was one of the most recent poets included by the compiler of the very first "Competition of The Thirty-six Women Poets" in the second half of the thirteenth century. In the imaginary portrait here she turns completely away. The only other rear-view pose in this set is that of Princess Shikishi in Round 1, who, as a Heian princess, might be expected to be less publicly visible than the other poets. Although the decision to avoid showing Gotoba-in no Shimotsuke's face may be arbitrary, it results in one of the most striking visual compositions in this book. The mound of clothing is animated by the curve of her hair, the lifting of her fan (as if to suggest that she is speaking her poem at this moment), and the unnatural energy of wide angular ribbons. The large crest on her right sleeve, which is drawn without naturalistic care for the folds in the material, stands out, not only because it is the most blatantly a-historical feature of the garments in this book, but also because it seems to define this picture as the illustration of a dress, only incidentally containing a poet.

mishi hito no

keburi to narishi

yūbe yori

na zo mutsumashiki

Shiogama no ura

Paying attention

Do not cry so intensely,

Oh autumn crickets.

To the fitful sleep of the old,

Complaining, noisily

10ʟ / *Kodai no Kimi*

Kodai no Kimi was also known as Sanjō-in Nyōkurōdo sakon (the name used in the text of this book), which suggests that she held a position in the Office of Palace Women (*Nyōkurōdo*) at the time of Emperor Sanjō (976–1017; r. 1011–1016).[1] She probably died in the early eleventh century. Twenty of her poems are in imperial anthologies.

Kodai no Kimi was highly regarded as a poet in her lifetime, and had the distinction of being the most contemporary of only five women included by the poet and critic Fujiwara no Kintō in his list of the leading poets of Japan, The Thirty-six Immortal Poets, which he compiled around the year 1012. It was this list that inspired the later selection of The Thirty-six Immortal Women Poets represented in this competition.

This poem was included in the *Shinkokin wakashu*[2] in the section of love poems with this headnote: "Thinking that she would send a pomander to a woman, she took the place of a man and wrote this poem." The poem was written for the fifth day of the fifth month, the Sweet-flag Festival, aimed at warding off disease by gathering and using aromatics. On this day it was customary to hang pomanders, small brocade balls filled with fragrant materials, particularly sweet-flag roots, and decorated with artificial flowers and long strings in five colors. The poem was attached to one of these pomanders when it was sent to the woman. The most desirable roots are long and, consequently, comparable to deep affection. But there is also a hint of complaint in the poem in the reference to wet sleeves. The persona that Kodai no Kimi has adopted is that of a man who wants to suggest that he is more faithful than the woman he loves. In the anthology of Kodai no Kimi's poems, the anonymous woman's answer is recorded:[3]

kurushiki ni	What are you seeking
nani motomuramu	With so much pain and effort?
ayamegusa	Haven't you heard that
Asaka no numa ni	Sweet-flag plants are growing
ou to koso kike	In the pond at Asaka?

Asaka was associated with sweet-flag because of a poem in the *Kokin wakashū* (KKS 677). The woman's reply follows a tradition of dismissal and disbelief in response to protestations of love by men.

The male persona taken by Kodai no Kimi, the analogy of devotion and sweet-flag roots, the reference to poetic geography, and the clever reply seem particularly artificial. They remind us that the world of classical Japanese verse, like any sophisticated, high art, was a world of its own, with rules and systems that sometimes reignite and sometimes abandon the reality that inspires it.

numagoto ni
sode zo nurekeru
ayamegusa
kokoro ni nitaru
ne o motomu tote

In pond after pond
The sleeves of my robe were drenched!
Since I wanted to find
Roots of the sweet-flag that could
Match my affection for you

10ʀ / *Gotoba-in no Shimotsuke*

女

一ゝ坪にそのうちやか
さそらしていくる
かほき
くらかきや花る
れ花れ
弥さめ
小
す

後花園町西川流筆二翁書

10L / *Kodai no Kimi*

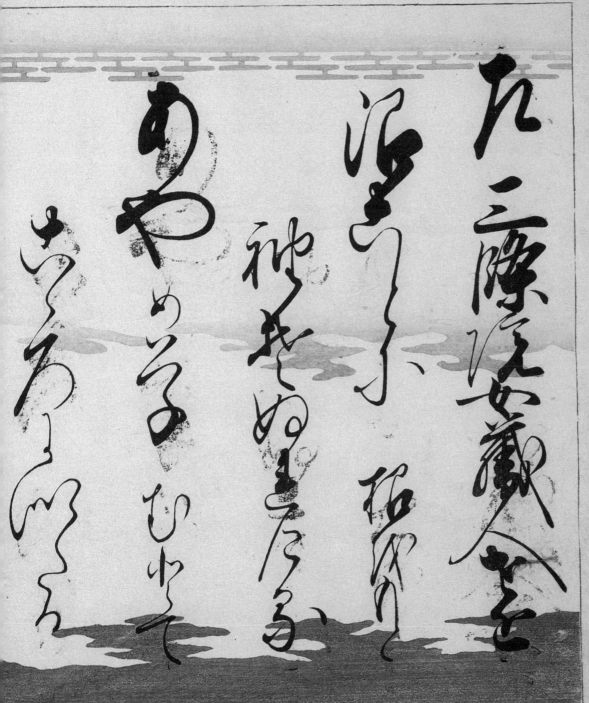

鉄砲町　會田ゆ□□女十一□□玄

9R / *Kojijū*

Kojijū was active in the second half of the twelfth century. In 1161, when she is thought to have been around forty years of age, she went to court to serve Emperor Nijō. After he died she served Empress Tashi (1140–1201) and then Emperor Takakura (1161–1181; r. 1168–1180). She took vows in 1179. She was part of Retired Emperor Gotoba's poetry circle in her last years, and died in the very beginning of the thirteenth century, probably in her eighties. Fifty-three of her poems are in imperial anthologies.

This poem was included in the *Shinkokin wakashū*, in the Miscellaneous section, with this headnote: "Composed as part of an offering of one hundred poems, on the subject of the feelings in a mountain retreat."[1] The set was composed in the year 1200, when Kojijū was an elderly nun, and she takes "mountain retreat" (*sanka*) to refer to a remote temple where one maintains a rigorous schedule of religious practice. The leaves that she picks are from an evergreen called *shikimi*, and are used as an offering on Buddhist altars. "Ink-dyed" (*sumizome*) refers to her black habit, and *oki* ("arose") describes the formation of dew as well as the act of waking.

At this point in the competition, Kojijū's verse is a welcome relief from love poetry and laments, and it seems nicely direct and simple. But the tradition of classical Japanese poetry is so long and involved that even such clarity has its unspoken implications. For hundreds of years and thousands of poems before this one, sleeves were drenched with tears of sorrow or frustration, mountain paths led to hidden ladies, dew recalled the evanescence of life and the emptiness of promises, and dawn was the time of parting. By excluding all these standard allusions from the poem, Kojijū is expressing the essential nature of her religious vocation. She has deliberately left behind the desires and disappointments of secular life, including the emotions surrounding love. Now dew is just dew.

The two poems in this round show a sharp contrast between a worldly woman, famous for her love life, who is closely linked to the past even when she has thought it buried, and a detached, religious woman, so removed from the emotions of the world that, even if she thinks of the past, she is most affected by the fact that she rises early. Like each round in the competition, this juxtaposition is itself an artistic statement by the compiler, the result of careful selection from hundreds of possible poems.

shikimi tsumu

yamaji no tsuyu ni

nurenikeri

akatsuki oki no

sumizome no sode

Now they have been drenched

By dew on the mountain path

Where I pick green leaves.

These ink-dyed sleeves of mine

That arose in dawn's light

9L / *Izumi Shikibu*

Izumi Shikibu (ca. 975–1027–?), like Murasaki Shikibu, served Empress Shōshi. She was married to Tachibana no Michisada, by whom she had a daughter, Koshikibu (literally, "little Shikibu"). Koshikibu, generally known as Koshikibu no naishi, was also a poet, and appears in Round 12 of this competition. Until she died around the age of twenty-six, she too served Shōshi. Izumi Shikibu had famous affairs with Prince Tametaka (977–1002)—which probably led to her divorce from Michisada—and, after Tametaka died, with Prince Atsumichi (981–1007). She also married Fujiwara no Yasumasa (958–1036). Murasaki Shikibu wrote in her diary:

> Now someone who did carry on a fascinating correspondence was Izumi Shikibu. She does have a rather unsavory side to her character but has a genius for tossing off letters with ease and can make the most banal statement sound special. Her poems are quite delightful. Although her knowledge of the canon and her judgments leave something to be desired, she can produce poems at will and always manages to include some clever phrase or other that catches the eye, and yet when it comes to criticizing or judging the work of others, well, she never really comes up to scratch; the sort of person who relies on a talent for extemporization, one feels. I cannot think of her as a poet of the highest quality.[1]

Later readers, better able to separate Izumi Shikibu's personality from her poetry, have had a better opinion of her work: she is represented in imperial anthologies by two hundred forty poems, more than any other woman and all but a few men. (Only fifty-nine of Murasaki's poems were included in those prestigious collections.) Izumi Shikibu's fictionalized diary, *Izumi shikibu nikki*, is one of the classics of Heian literature.[2]

This poem appeared in the Miscellaneous section of the imperial anthology *Kin'yō wakashū*, compiled by Minamoto no Toshiyori (1055–1129) around 1127. The headnote reads: "After Koshikibu died, Jotōmon-in [Shōshi] still sent robes to her as she had done for years in the past. When Izumi Shikibu saw the name 'Koshikibu no naishi' written down and attached to them, she composed this poem."[3]

Izumi Shikibu's pain over her daughter's death is renewed by the sight of her name. Like the written name, her love for her daughter was not buried with her and does not diminish. In a subtle way the poem is as much about remembering and forgetting as it is about loss and love.[4]

morotomo ni
koke no shita ni wa
kuchizu shite
uzumorenu na wo
miru zo kanashiki

This name of hers,
Not buried together with her,
And not decaying
Underneath the moss, oh,
Seeing it brings such sorrow!

右　小侍従

撓つひすめを
つゆりのめり
めよ篠小
めんよ
雷て
あつき
めらの

かうや町　長谷川れめ十二本て

9L / *Izumi Shikibu*

たいゝ闇しきぬ

うはと三波
みつもり

きみを名を
そばふち

みかてゆる
かける

まらす
ゝく

作田豊人町　立里て窓　女十一景妻

8R / *Nijō-in no Sanuki*

Nijō-in no Sanuki (1141–1217) served Emperor Nijō (1143–1165; r. 1158–1165) until his death. She then married Fujiwara no Shigeyori and bore two boys and a girl. She returned to court in the service of Empress Ninshi in the 1190s (where she worked with Gishūmon-in no Tango), and took vows after Ninshi's death in 1196. She too was active in the poetry circle around Retired Emperor Gotoba. Seventy of her poems are in imperial anthologies.

Like the poem it is paired with, this verse was included in the *Senzai wakashū*, but in the category of Love and with this headnote: "composed as a love poem."[1] Its theme is one of the classic subjects of Japanese love poetry: the loneliness and sorrow of a woman whom a man has ceased to visit. His faithlessness in this case is particularly blatant, since she feels that he never even intended to return after the first night. The two keys words that evoke this sad situation are *yogare* ("to break off relations") and *samushiro* ("narrow mat"). Both words have a long and special history in love poetry. A more general term, *yagate mo* ("just as it was"), here is used to refer both to the dust and to the woman who is speaking.

Since this poem is about love, it tempts us to read Akazome Emon's poem in the first half of the round as describing a similar situation. Without the context that was provided by the *Senzai wakashū* headnote and exchange, Akazome Emon's poem could also be seen as the complaint of an abandoned woman. Japanese poems, because of their tendency to ambiguity and allusion, are frequently assigned new meanings by being repositioned in fresh contexts. The words remain the same but their emotional significance changes. Akazome Emon's poem of tender sympathy in the *Senzai wakashū* could be seen as a poem of bitter complaint in this competition.

Nijō-in no Sanuki's poem seems to me to be superior to Akazome Emon's verse, no matter what context we set it in. A well-known early-thirteenth-century poetry treatise cites Sanuki's work as an example of a poem that expresses its meaning directly.[2] An interesting contrast is an anonymous *Kokin wakashū* love poem that also is critical of lies and abandonment, but uses elegant indirection to chide an ardent visitor:[3]

taga sato ni	Whose nests
yogare o shite ka	Are you abandoning,
hototogisu	Oh cuckoo,
tada koko ni shi mo	Who sings to me that here
netaru koe suru	Is the only place you sleep.

hitoyo tote

yogareshi toko no

samushiro ni

yagate mo chiri no

tsumorinuru kana

On this narrow mat—

The bed where he abandoned me,

Thinking, 'just one night'—

Untouched, how the dirt and dust

Have now accumulated.

8L / *Akazome Emon*

Akazome Emon (ca. 957–1041?) was the wife of Ōe no Masahira (952–1012) and the daughter of an official in the Office of the Palace Guards (*Emon*). She was personally known to Murasaki Shikibu, who wrote of her: "She may not be a genius but she has great poise and does not feel that she has to compose a poem on everything she sees merely because she is a poet. From what I have seen, her work is most accomplished, even her occasional verse."[1] She was lady-in-waiting to Rinshi, wife of the most powerful man of the time, Fujiwara no Michinaga (966–1027), and later served his daughter Shōshi (988–1074). Michinaga saw to it that Shōshi was made empress while still a child. Murasaki Shikibu was also in attendance to Shōshi.

Akazome Emon took religious vows when her husband Masahira died. She was still composing poetry as late as 1041, and it is presumed that she died soon afterward, probably in her eighties. The anthology of her complete works contains over six hundred poems. She is also said to be the author of *Eiga monogatari*,[2] a major historical narrative of the time. Ninety-six of her poems are in imperial anthologies.

This poem appears in the Laments section of the imperial anthology *Senzai wakashū*, compiled in 1188 by Fujiwara no Shunzei.[3] The headnote reads: "Having gone to Jotōmon Temple, she composed this poem on the morning after she saw Empress Shōshi, who had been thinking of her late husband, Emperor Ichijō." This contextual information clarifies our understanding of the poem, since it implies that Akazome Emon is not only expressing her own sorrow, but imagining as well the suffering of the empress. That is why her tears fall even more abundantly than before. Shunzei followed this poem in the *Senzai wakashū* with Empress Shōshi's response:

utsutsu to mo	I cannot decide
omoiwakarede	What is real and what is not.
suguru ma ni	How could I describe
mishi yo no yume o	The night dreams that I have seen
nani kataruran	In the time since he passed away?

The empress is so distressed that she has lost any sense of what is real. In her dreams, generated out of her desperate longing, the emperor is still present, just as was Ono no Komachi's lover in the first poem of this competition.

tsune yori mo

mata nuresoishi

tamoto kana

mukashi o kakete

otsuru namida ni

More than ever before
They were soaked through yet again,
Oh, these sleeves of mine,
By the tears that I have shed
Thinking of the distant past.

8R / *Nijō-in no Sanuki*

古

二條院讃岐

きもりろふ
ゆくくも

一

はるゝ
ゆくか
よゝゝゝ
しゝの

日市　吉田

8L / *Akazome Emon*

油田かつ卅ハ
竹内あきさ
十二家生

た　赤流滞つ

たゝひしりを
まゝ劣
　　むしノ
　　　まそ

ものし
まりと
おつふ
　　しのふ

7R / *Kayōmon-in no Echizen*

Kayōmon-in no Echizen lived in the first half of the thirteenth century and served Emperor Gotoba's mother, Shokushi, and his daughter, Kayōmon-in. She was part of the poetry circle around the Emperor Gotoba during the period of his retirement and the assembling of the *Shinkokin wakashū*. She was still writing poetry at least as late as 1248. Twenty-five of her poems are in imperial anthologies.

This poem was included in the *Shinkokin wakashū* with a simple headnote, "on the topic of long-lasting love."[1] It is directly based on an anonymous love poem in the *Kokin wakashū* that was written over three hundred years earlier:[2]

natsubiki no	In summer's spinning,
tebiki no ito o	Hand-spun threads are whirling
kurikaeshi	Around and around
koto shigekutomo	Rumors may run thickly but
taemu to omou na	Do not think of cutting this short.

Poets at the time of the *Shinkokin wakashū* looked to the *Kokin wakashū* from three centuries earlier as embodying the highest standards of court poetry. Consequently, many of the poems in the *Shinkokin wakashū* take *Kokin wakashū* poems as their models and inspiration. The anonymous poem above was probably part of an actual exchange between a man and a woman, in which the man has suggested breaking off their affair because others may learn of it, and the woman replies that she wishes to continue.[3] Kayōmon-in no Echizen's poem is an imaginary continuation of this exchange.

But her poem is even more a response to the art of the past than it is to a particular dialogue. The *Kokin wakashū* poem links the image of spinning thread with love through several double usages: *kurikaeshi*, "around and around" or "again and again," can refer to either the thread or the rumors; *koto* is either the "activity" of thread spinning or the "words" of gossip; *tae* is either to "cut" thread or to "end" a relationship. In fact, *kurikaeshi koto shige* acts as an extended pivot word (in translation: "...whirling around and around. Around and around rumors may run..."). Kayōmon-in no Echizen proves the level of her skill by keeping most of these double meanings and adding even more: the verb *fu* means either "to set up a loom with warp threads" or "to pass time," and *musubohore* is either "to tie a knot" or "to be depressed." There is no pivot word in Echizen's poem, however. Instead the paired possibilities of meaning all funnel down to the final word, in which both settings reach their climax. The thread is a tangle and the lady is depressed, and because this verb ends with a suffix, *tsutsu* (indicating ongoing or repetitive action), her frustration continues.

natsubiki no
tebiki no ito no
toshi futomo
taenu omoi ni
musubohoretsutsu

Though our years stretch out
In even line like hand-spun thread
In summer's spinning, yet,
In a love that will not be cut
We ourselves are now so tangled . . .

7L / *Uma no naishi*

Uma no naishi was probably born around the middle of the tenth century. She served a long series of high court ladies,[1] and was an older contemporary of Sei Shōnagon (see Round 14). Uma no naishi took Buddhist vows near the end of her life and retired to a temple in the country. Thirty-seven of her poems are in imperial anthologies. This one was selected for the Love section of the *Shinkokin wakashū*[2] with this headnote: "After Left Captain [Fujiwara] Asatera had not visited in a long time, he went to meet her at a place to which she had traveled. Because there was no pillow, she made one of bound grasses and composed this poem."

The poem hinges on two double meanings: *tabi* in *kagiri no tabi* is both "our final time" and "our final journey"; *kare* (here pronounced *gare*) in *shimogarenikeri* is both "withered (by frost)" and "estranged (by you)." The wordplay with *tabi* does not add much to the poem, but *shimogarenikeri* is very evocative, both of the dead, fragile stalks of straw and the withered, cold state of their relationship. It is accusatory since it associates Asatera with the killing frost. Although the noun *shimogare*, "frost-withered," is at least as old as the *Man'yōshū*, it came to be used in poetry as a verb only in Uma no naishi's time, and its metaphorical use here is the poem's creative feature.

The calligraphic arrangement of the poem on the page is a restrained version of what is known as "scattered writing" (*chirashigaki*), because the words are not organized neatly from top to bottom, right to left. The dark characters in the first line on the right are the team designation (at the top) and the poet's name (at the bottom). The poem begins with the dark writing of the third line (from the right) and continues through the fourth, fifth, and sixth lines (consisting of only one character at the bottom left corner), with each line starting at a level lower than the last. But these lines account for only the first part of the poem, plus the word *kusa* from the beginning of the second part (*kusa*, "grass," is the lone character at the bottom left). The calligrapher has now worked herself down into the corner but has written only slightly over half the poem. So she goes back to the remaining empty spaces to put the rest of the words wherever there is a convenient space. While these choices of spacing and positioning are primarily aesthetic, the scattered writing style had its origin in the practical problem of the Heian correspondent, who had to put a complete letter on a single page that could be nicely folded for delivery, but who did not know in advance how much space would be needed, and consequently had to keep going back to slip in more words wherever there was room.

au koto wa
kore ya kagiri no
tabi naramu
kusa no makura mo
shimogarenikeri

Now we have met, but
Will it be the final time
We are together?
Even my pillow of grass
Is withered and dead from frost.

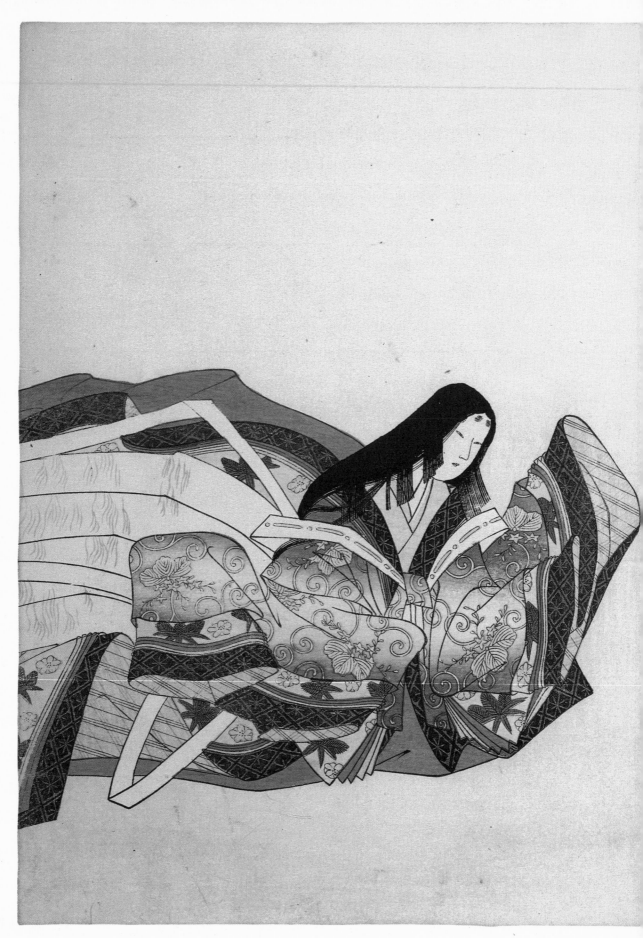

7R / *Kayōmon-in no Echizen*

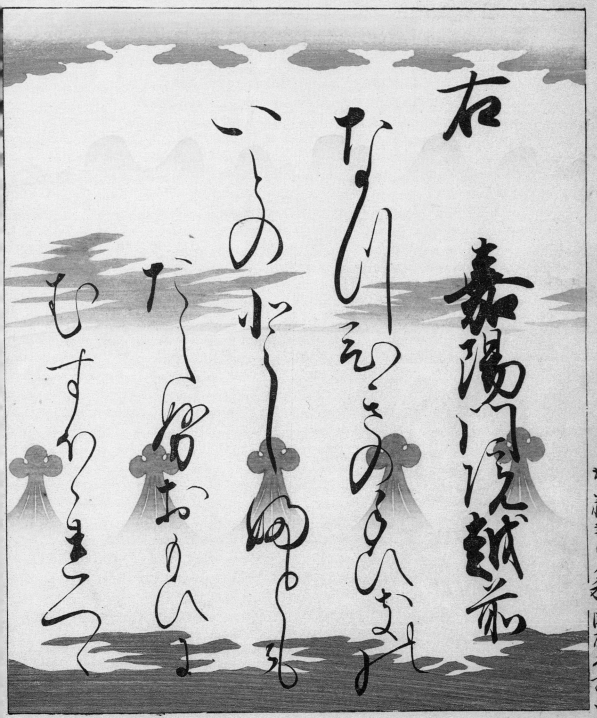

右　泰陽門院越前

なか月
…の…

いその水…
…ぬ…

たゝ…おりは
むすひ…て

平荘きつ／龍岡屋…十四葉事

7L / *Uma no naishi*

たれし

の柳を

あやめ

の

馬のは

草枯たよ

かきつはた

李

の蛇

うしも

小あ〜四〜二目小杉きり女十一第季

6R / *Gishūmon-in no Tango*

Gishūmon-in no Tango was active in the poetry circles around Emperor Gotoba and served his consort, Empress Ninshi (1173–1238). The poet took Buddhist vows and retired from court life in 1201, but continued writing poetry at least until 1208. Forty-six of her poems are in imperial anthologies.

This poem appears in the Miscellaneous section of the *Shinkokin wakashū*, but without a headnote.[1] The phrase *koke no tamoto*, "sleeves of moss," like *koke no koromo*, "robes of moss," came to be used in the poetry of monks and nuns. The starting point for this tradition was a poem by the priest Henjō (816–890) in the *Kokin wakashū*.[2] Henjō had left court life and taken vows when his patron, Emperor Ninmyō (810–850; r. 833–850), died and a year later, after the mourning period ended, he wrote this poem at his temple retreat outside the city:

mina hito wa	Everyone, I hear,
hana no koromo ni	Has now changed back into their
narinu nari	Robes of blossoms.
koke no tamoto yo	Oh, you my sleeves of moss,
kawaki dani se yo	Could you not at least dry out?

Henjō uses moss to combine the idea of the simplicity of his priestly garb with the suggestion that his tears of loss are constant. Gishūmon-in no Tango, three hundred years later, returns the moss to the woods in her last two lines, which refer equally to the poet's wet sleeves and the forest floor.[3]

Gishūmon-in no Tango composed this poem as part of an actual poetry competition held in 1204. Thirty leading poets of the time participated in composing verse on three topics: falling leaves, moon at dawn, and wind in the pines. The judgments were made by the consensus of all the participants and recorded by Fujiwara no Teika. Gishūmon-in no Tango had the third position on the Right team and was paired opposite the male poet Fujiwara no Tadayoshi (1164–1225). She won against him in two rounds and tied one.

This poem was one of her winning entries. The competing verse was the following:

sabishisa o	Even if I grow used
taenu nagame ni	To brooding that does not end
naraite mo	My lonely sadness
nao yūgure no	The wind that still blows
matsu ni fuku kaze	Through the pines at evening...

Teika recorded the judgment: "The phrase 'Back and forth over sleeves of moss / The sweeping wind through the pines' sounds very fine, and we can make this poem the winner."[4]

nani to naku

kikeba namida zo

koborekeru

koke no tamoto ni

kayou matsukaze

Somehow or other

When I hear it, oh, the tears

How they pour out!

Back and forth over sleeves of moss

The sweeping wind through the pines

6L / *Michitsuna no haha*

Michitsuna no haha (ca. 936–995), "mother of [Fujiwara] Michitsuna," is one of the most important writers of the Heian period. She is the author of *Kagerō nikki*, a literary autobiography that covers the period from 954 to 974, focusing on her deteriorating relationship with her husband, Fujiwara no Kaneie (929–990), a leading political figure of the time.[1] She was also highly regarded as a poet, and thirty six of her poems appear in imperial anthologies.

This poem appears in *Kagerō nikki*, and was also included in the Love section of the *Shinkokin wakashū*, with this headnote: "At a time when the Retired Chancellor [Kaneie] had not visited in a long while, she was combing her hair and took out a basin to wet it with. She composed this poem about what she saw as she was putting water in it."[2]

The description of the setting is more complete in *Kagerō nikki*.[3] Kaneie had come to spend the day with her, and after some casual conversation she started to criticize him. Kaneie was offended and stalked off, saying he would not return. After five or six days she began to worry that he might have been serious. She noticed that the basin of rice-cooking water that he had been using to set his hair the day he left was still in the room, but with a layer of dust on the surface of the water. Suddenly she realized with dismay how long it had been since he had visited, and she composed this poem. On that very day he came back, behaving as if nothing had happened.

The basin of water is used as a symbol of domestic harmony, because setting one's hair by combing rice water through it is an intimate act that would be shared only with a personal servant and immediate family. Here the poet is trapped by her husband's moods. If she complains of his neglect, he punishes her by neglecting her more.

This poem works so well because there is little internal redundancy and because the key words have complex and reinforcing connotations. The first word, for example, *tae*, is used to describe the death of living things as well as the end of a relationship, while the final line, *mikusa inikeri*,[4] "water-weed grows," implies an abundant growth, but one that follows from neglect.[5]

The depressing implication of water-weed can be traced back to this poem by Yamabe no Akahito (eighth century), inspired by the decrepit garden of a once-famous aristocrat:[6]

inishie no	Here at this ruin
furuki tokoro wa	Left from the distant past
toshi fukami	Due to the weight of years
ike no nagisa ni	How the water-weed has grown
mikusa oinikeri	On the edges of the pond.

taenuru ka
kage dani mieba
toubeki ni
katami no mizu wa
mikusa inikeri

Have we come to the end?
If you appeared, even in reflection,
That is what I would ask.
But on the pool of remembrance
How the water-weed has grown!

6R / *Gishūmon-in no Tango*

六　宣秋院御母

家ちかく
なみのよするを
そのままに
かけて
かよふや
一つ松風

富沢町南閤軒五十三郎書

6L / *Michitsuna no haha*

た

小伝馬町二丁目豊田☡☡☡中☡書

右大将道綱母

嘆きつゝ
ひとりぬる夜の
あくるまは
いかにひさしき
ものとかはしる

5R / *Taikenmon-in no Horikawa*

Taikenmon-in no Horikawa was an attendant to the consort of Emperor Toba (1103–1156; r. 1107–1123), Empress Shōshi (1101–1145), who was known as Taikenmon-in. The poet's exact dates are not known, but she took Buddhist vows after Empress Shōshi did in 1142. Sixty-five of her poems are included in imperial anthologies. This poem was published in the *Senzai wakashū* with this headnote: "On an occasion when one hundred poems were offered, this one was composed on the subject of love."[1]

It is a striking contrast to the poem by Ukon with which it is paired in the competition. The previous verse was dense with double-meaning words, complex syntactic intertwinings, and a surprising wealth of images. Taikenmon-in no Horikawa's poem has few physical references, either explicit or implicit, uses common vocabulary, and follows a straightforward grammar. Except for its meter, syllable length, and division into two parts, it could be mistaken for prose.

This poetry competition contains no judgments and no judge, but the compiler who selected these poems to represent these poets used considerable care. By presenting them in a competition rather than in a selection or series, the compiler has given each reader an opportunity to take on a critical role. Taikenmon-in no Horikawa's poem may seem more direct in expression than Ukon's, but it is not simple. When the lady of the poem wonders why her feelings too have changed, she recognizes that she is, in fact, no less susceptible to the loss of interest than he is. One might call this rhetorical complexity, in contrast to the syntactic complexity of Ukon's poem.

But both poems are interesting because they end with suggestions of self-doubt. Ukon's narrator seems to have every reason to feel angry and yet she holds back. The speaker in the second poem has already passed beyond an emotional reaction to her lover's fickle nature and is now wondering why in fact she is behaving the same way he does.

The arrangement of the calligraphy in the text of Taikenmon-in no Horikawa's poem is a good example of diagonal ordering. The right-hand column of the page contains the team designation ("right") at the top, directly above the name of the poet. The poem begins to the left and just slightly below the starting point of the name with *uki hito o*. It continues again to the left and slightly down for four more lines (through *omoiki ya*) until it has worked itself into the corner. Part two of the poem begins at the top of the page, just left of the team designation, and slides quickly down to the left with no more than a syllable or two per line. By the time it is down in the corner it is as far as *kawaru* and so the final two syllables, *ramu*, are placed in the upper left corner. The placement is conscious of the structure of the poem, because it clearly distinguishes the upper part (the first three measures) and the lower part (the final two measures).

uki hito o
shinobubeshi to wa
omoiki ya
waga kokoro sae
nado kawaruramu

Did I once think
That I would long for
That faithless man?
Now this heart of mine—
Why has it too changed?

5L / *Ukon*

Ukon was a minor poet of the tenth century. She served the Empress Onshi and is thought to have been the daughter of Fujiwara no Suetsuna (d. 919). She is known to have participated in several poetry competitions in the 960s. Nine of her poems are in imperial anthologies. This poem uses *koyu* as a pivot word representing both a verb and a proper name: ". . .months passed. Past-rock Shore . . ." It appeared in the *Gosen wakashū* with the headnote "Because a man did not visit for a long time."[1]

The poem is more complex than translation allows. It contains three main parts. The first is a straightforward, proselike statement: *au koto o matsu ni tsukihi wa koyu* ("months passed as I waited to see you"). The second reuses the two syllables of *koyu* and describes an apparently unrelated physical scene: *Koyurugi no iso ni idete ya* ("if I leave for Koyurugi Shore"). And the third ties the two together with a double-meaning phrase that applies to both: *ima wa uramimu* ("now I feel resentful") and *ima wa ura mimu* ("now I see the bay").

Word breaks are not ordinarily signaled in classical Japanese by the text itself; hence, it is impossible to distinguish visually between the verb *urami* ("to feel resentful") and the noun-verb group *ura* ("bay") *mi* ("to see"). In this final line the first meaning is the primary one, since it works best with *ima wa* ("and now").

In this way the poem comprises two separate ideas intertwined by *koyu* and *urami*: "you didn't come to see me and I hate you for it," and "if I go to Koyurugi Shore, I'll see the bay." The juxtaposition is ambiguous, because there is no direct linkage between the two other than the pivot word. In the literary theory of the time, it was understood that poems should bring together the emotional experience of the poet and the physical realities of nature. But each reader was expected to resolve the details of this relationship personally. My attention is drawn to two other images hidden in the words: *matsu*, which means "pines" as well as "wait," and *tsuki*, "moon," in the first part of the word *tsukihi*, "months and days." The word that I have translated as "Shore," *iso*, implies an abundance of rocks (as does the *gi* in *Koyurugi*). Pine trees on a rocky shore are usually battered by the weather, and I resolve this juxtaposition by visualizing a turbulent, hard, cold, and remote setting that mirrors the loneliness of the woman waiting pointlessly night after night.

au koto o
matsu ni tsukihi wa
Koyurugi no
iso ni idete ya
ima wa uramimu

Waiting for you to
Come to me, how the months have
Past-rock Shore—If I
Went out there now, would the name
Itself provoke resentment?

5R / *Taikenmon-in no Horikawa*

右　待賢門院堀河

ながからむ心もしらず

くろかみのみだれてけさは

ものをこそおもへ

室町二百　山田業清わ十二歳書

5L / *Ukon*

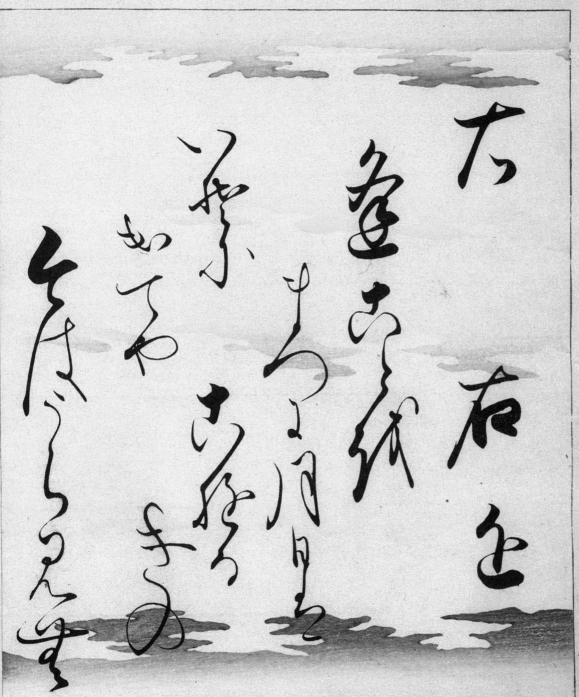

右左を

小伝馬町二丁目　豊田義信女　□衆書

4R / *Shunzei no musume*

Shunzei no musume ("daughter of Shunzei") (1171?–1254) was born the daughter of Fujiwara no Moriyori and his wife, Hachijō-in no Sanjō, who was the daughter of Fujiwara no Shunzei (1114–1204). At a young age she was adopted by her grandfather Shunzei, perhaps because her father was implicated in a political disturbance in 1177. Around 1190 she married Fujiwara no Michitomo; they had a son and a daughter, but after about ten years they separated, and in 1213 she took Buddhist vows. She was first recognized as a poet by Emperor Gotoba, who included her as a key female member of his poetry circle, and she was active as a poet throughout her long life. Princess Shikishi, Kunaikyō, and Shunzei no musume are generally recognized today as the greatest women poets of the early thirteenth century. One hundred nine of her poems are included in imperial anthologies.

This poem appeared in the Love section of the *Shinkokin wakashū* with the headnote "Composed on the subject of love in spring, for the competition of fifteen poems on love that was held at Minase."[1]

Retired Emperor Gotoba was the sponsor of this competition, held in 1202. The emperor handed down a set of fifteen topics, all on love, such as spring love, dawn love, seashore love, love using rain imagery, and so on. Only ten poets participated, among whom Shunzei no musume and Kunaikyō were the only women. Fujiwara no Shunzei was the judge. Each poet composed his or her entries independently over about a one-week period, and, except for Shunzei no musume, Kunaikyō, and one other poet, the participants came together for the judging. Shunzei no musume was positioned as leader of the Left team and was paired against Shunzei's son, the great poet Fujiwara no Teika (1162–1241), who led the Right team. This poem won its round.

It is an imagistic poem composed of strong words, each of which has a rich, evocative history in Japanese poetry. The most direct allusion, however, is to one of the most famous poems in the tradition, composed by Ariwara no Narihira (825–880). Narihira had been secretly visiting a woman who suddenly disappeared from the palace where she had worked. One night he went to her empty room and composed this poem as he lay on the floor looking at the spring full moon:[2]

tsuki ya aranu	This is not that moon.
haru ya mukashi no	And this spring is not that spring
haru naranu	Of long ago.
wagami hitotsu wa	While only I myself
moto no mi ni shite	Am just as I was before...

omokage no

kasumeru tsuki zo

yadorikeru

haru ya mukashi no

sode no namida ni

This moon by which

I once faintly saw you

Now comes to rest.

In the teardrops on my sleeve

For that spring of long ago

4L / *Saigū no nyōgo*

Saigū no nyōgo (929–985) was known in her lifetime as a calligrapher and musician as well as a poet.[1] Forty-one of her poems are in imperial anthologies.

The translation of this poem reproduces in English one of the inventions of Japanese poetry, a feature called the "pivot word" (*kakekotoba*). The word "suffer" (*uki*) does double duty, once with what precedes it, and once with what follows it: "We suffer. Suffering fills the world." A Japanese reader recognizes pivot words when the statement stops making sense exactly at the point where a word can be used in two ways.

This poem was selected for the Love section of the *Shinkokin wakashū*, where it appears with this headnote: "In the reign of Emperor Murakami she composed this poem in response to the phrase 'far apart.'"[2] This phrase, *madō ni are ya*, is a line in an older, anonymous poem:[3]

suma no ama no	The salt-making clothes
shioyakigoromo	Of Suma fisherwomen
osa o arami	Are roughly woven
madō ni are ya	Of threads so apart are we.
kimi ga kimasanu	Is that why you will not come?

The key word, *madō*, "far apart," has two meanings: it describes the gaps between the threads in the rough weave as well as the physical distance between the lady and her man. It is used here as a pivot word: "...threads so apart. So apart are we...."

Saigū no nyōgo's poem not only reproduces the double usage of *madō* ("far apart") and *uki* ("suffer"), but adds yet another double-meaning word, *nare*, ("close, familiar"), which can refer either to the relations between men and women or to the well-worn nature of a favorite garment. An old poem that used *nare* as a pivot word is this verse by the eighth-century poet Yamabe no Akahito:[4]

suma no ama no	The salt-making clothes
shioyakikinu no	Of Suma fisherwomen
narenaba ka	Are so familiar
hitohi mo kimi o	Are we that not for one day
wasurete omowamu	Could I fail to think of you.

Again we need to understand "familiar" twice: "... are so familiar. So familiar are we..." The device of the pivot word was especially popular in the ninth and tenth centuries, and allowed poets to create allusive juxtapositions that were justified not by meaning but by this odd structural tie. The only direct link between the fisherwomen's clothes and the love relationship is the double usage of a word like "far apart" or "familiar" as a pivot word. But there is also the implication that somehow being in love is not unlike the miserable life of a poor fisherwoman who doesn't even have decent clothes to wear.

156

nareyukeba

ukiyo nareba ya

Suma no ama no

shioyakigoromo

madō naruramu

When we become close

We suffer-ing fills the world,

So we are far apart

Threads in the salt-making robes

Of the fisherwoman at Suma.

4R / *Shunzei no musume*

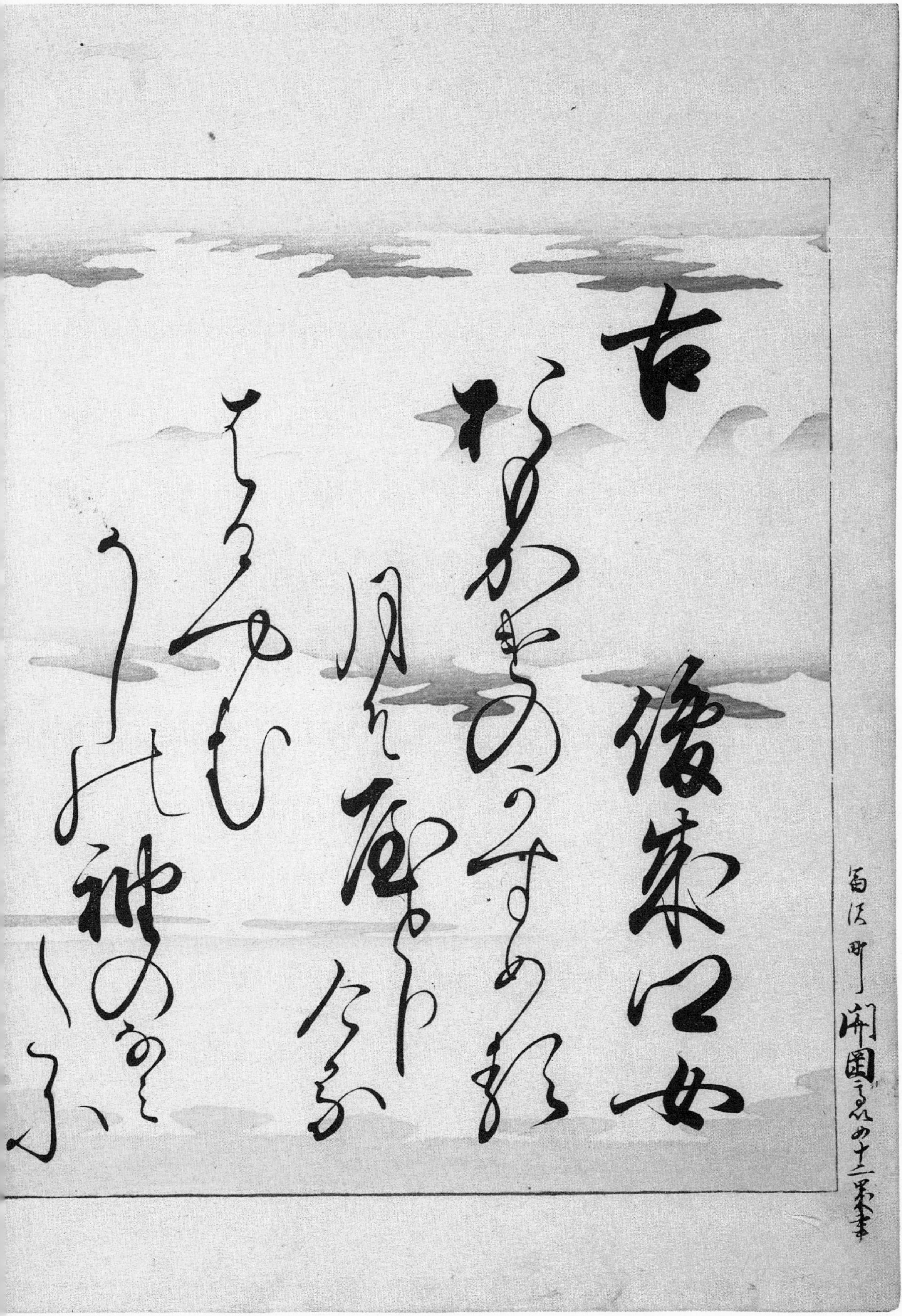

古

俊成口女

なには江の
月のよそなる
うらなれや
すむとも
みえぬ
あまの
たくなは

石清水
開闢うんぬ
十二第巻書

4L / *Saigū no nyōgo*

右うた キツメ
内野く前 半五夏舎

3R / *Suō no naishi*

Suō no naishi, whose given name was Chūshi, was the daughter of the eleventh-century poet Taira no Munenaka. She was called Suō no naishi because her father was once governor of Suō Province and she was an attendant (*naishi*). She first came to court to serve Emperor Goreizei (1025–1068; r. 1045–1068), but after he died she left; she was called back to serve Emperor Gosanjō (1034–1073; r. 1068–1072). Subsequently she was in attendance to two more emperors, Shirakawa (1053–1128; r. 1072–1086) and Horikawa (1079–1107; r. 1086–1107). She probably died around 1108–1112 after an unusually long career at court. Thirty-five of her poems are in imperial anthologies. This poem was selected for the Love section of the imperial anthology *Goshūi wakashū* (compiled in 1086) with the headnote "Sent to a man whose feelings had changed."[1]

As with Nakatsukasa's poem, a man has stopped visiting and the lady writes to express her sorrow and to request a reappearance. Both of these poems were so suggestive that they inspired important later verses. Nakatsukasa's poem gave rise to this verse by Anbō hōshi no musume, the daughter of Anbō, a Buddhist priest and poet who lived in the late tenth century:[2]

yo no tsune no	If this autumn wind
akikaze naraba	Is the typical one,
ogi no ha ni	Among the reed grass,
soyo to bakari no	Even if just a whisper,
oto wa shitemashi	It ought to produce some sound.

This time the poet suggests that the man is the autumn wind, using yet another double meaning well beloved by Japanese poets: *aki* the noun is "autumn," but *aki* the verb is "to be fed up with" or "to be tired of." The man, she implies, has typically reached the stage where he is tired of her. But at least he should send some word, or make one more visit, however short.[3]

Suō no naishi's poem inspired Princess Shikishi (see Round 1):[4]

tsuraku tomo	Despite the distress
sate shi mo hateji	I will not end it like this.
chigirishi ni	Because a heart
aranu kokoro mo	That has not pledged its love
sadamenakereba	Is still not beyond changing.

Sequences of reinterpretations, variations, and echoes like these kept enriching the allusive power of these short poems over hundreds of years, until just the mention of a phrase like *ogi no ha* ("reed grass") or *chigirishi ni aranu* ("unpledged love") could ignite a chain of images and emotions.

chigirishi ni
aranu tsurasa mo
au koto no
naki ni wa e koso
uramizarikere

This distress because
You have not pledged your love—
If I am never
To see you again, how
Can I complain of it?

3L / *Nakatsukasa*

Nakatsukasa was the daughter of the poet Ise (see Round 2) and Prince Atsuyoshi, who was son of Emperor Uda and held the title Nakatsukasakyō. She was married to Minamoto no Nobuakira, but had relations with a number of men. She was writing poetry by the 950s and lived at least until 989. Sixty of her poems are in imperial anthologies. This poem was included in the Love section of the *Gosen wakashū*, the imperial anthology ordered in 951, with this headnote: "When Taira Kaneki was gradually becoming estranged from her, she sent him this poem."[1]

Nakatsukasa's poem recalls an anonymous poem that was included in the earlier anthology *Kokin wakashū*:[2]

higurashi no	Sunset cicadas
naku yamazato no	Cry in the mountain village
yūgure wa	As evening falls
kaze yori hoka ni	And aside from the wind
tou hito mo nashi	No one comes to visit.

Each of these lines contains at least one image associated with sadness in autumn: cicadas, cry, mountain village, evening, wind, and no visitor. Nakatsukasa echoes this sad setting in the first three lines of her poem, but in the final two lines she makes her statement personal by comparing her lover to the reed grasses. The sound of the newly withered reed grasses blowing in the breeze is treated in poetry as a sign of the onset of lonely autumn. She hears from the grasses, but not from him. However, anyone who has read thousands of autumn poems, as he presumably has, would also know that a favorite double meaning in love poetry was contained in the word *kare*, which means "withered" when applied to things like grasses, but "estranged" when used in reference to love. Although the word *kare* is not present in the poem, it is introduced indirectly through the rustling dead grasses and through a rich train of associations that evolved within earlier poetry. In this interpretation, the phrase "if you were a reed grass" is a disguised way of saying "if you are leaving me." Was he so impressed by her delicacy and sensitivity that he gave up the thought of leaving her? Unfortunately, no response has been preserved.

In the tenth century the role that poetry played in the relations between men and women of the court was still important. It allowed words to bear complex implications and connotations acquired through a shared literary tradition, and so permitted a concentration of meaning in the rather confined space of thirty-one syllables. This same brevity also permitted ambiguity, which poets used in order to suggest what they might not dare to say directly.

akikaze no

fuku ni tsukete mo

towanu kana

ogi no ha naraba

oto wa shitemashi

No visitor comes

Along with the blowing

Of this autumn wind.

If you were a reed grass,

You ought to produce some sound.

3R / *Suō no naishi*

古 関路内侍

舟つて
 いのを
にてし岸

あまの
たちの
なすにも
えしを

3L / *Nakatsukasa*

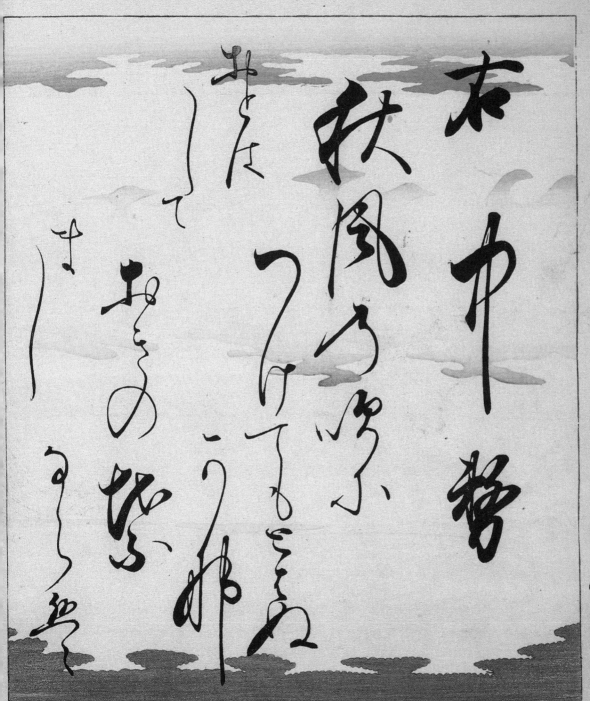

右巾幗

秋風乃涼
つけてもこゝぬ
またはしてまたに
をまのつゝく
はしまうろく

光井一町神山…を象せ十五家書

2ʀ / *Kunaikyō*

Kunaikyō was a poet-prodigy who, in a career of only five years, from 1200 to 1204, was regarded as one of the important poets of her time. She is thought to have died in 1204 or 1205 at around the age of twenty or younger. Her mother, Aki, a famous koto player, was the daughter of court painter Kose no Muneshige and an attendant to Emperor Goshirakawa. Her father was a mid-level bureaucrat, Minamoto no Moromitsu. Kunaikyō came to court to serve Emperor Gotoba (1180–1239; r. 1183–1198), who was himself an accomplished poet and the force behind the compilation of the *Shinkokin wakashū*. She is also known as Gotoba-in no Kunaikyō. Forty-three of her poems are in imperial anthologies. This poem is found in the Spring section of the *Shokukokin wakashū* with the headnote "A poem on cherry blossoms."[1]

The beginning of the poem sets a scene of early spring. As the poet looks out into the distance, she sees cherry trees starting to blossom everywhere in the low-lying valley, but not yet on the mountains. Effortlessly, at the end of the verse, the subject shifts and our focus is now Yoshino Mountain, the one place where the trees are not in bloom, although it is the most famous place for cherry blossoms.

The poet describes Mount Yoshino with the unusual phrase *hana mo oku aru*, which takes a familiar word with many meanings and connotations, *oku*, and applies it in a completely original way. Fundamentally *oku* means "interior," the opposite of the entrance or edge of something, and implies invisible mystery and spiritual power. It is frequently used in combination with *yama*, "mountain," to form *okuyama*, "the deep, remote mountains." By extension, when applied to time it means the limit or end of something, the farthest point, the ultimate, unseen future. Applying this powerful word to cherry blossoms (*hana*) reminds us that however lovely the scene of early blossoms may be now, once the trees on Yoshino Mountain come into bloom it will be truly spectacular. But it also suggests that the blossoms have taken sanctuary deep in the holy mountain. Yoshino Mountain was a sacred site as well as a scenic beauty spot, and for centuries religious ascetics had gone there to carry out rigorous spiritual training. What started as another harmless poem on pretty cherry blossoms somehow manages in its short span to generate successive waves of suggestive meaning that reach into the deepest levels (*oku*) of experience.

miwataseba

fumoto bakari ni

sakisomete

hana mo oku aru

Miyoshino no yama

Everywhere I look

Cherry trees are starting to bloom,

Right up to the base

Of lovely Mount Yoshino

Whose blossoms are still deep within.

2L / *Ise*

Ise was the daughter of Fujiwara no Tsugukage, who served as a governor of Ise Province (appointed in 885) and Yamato Province (from 891 to 895). She was called Ise probably because she first went to court when her father was governor of Ise. She served as an attendant to Empress Onshi (872–907), consort of Emperor Uda (867–931; r. 887–897). She had an affair with Onshi's brother Fujiwara no Nakahira (875–945) that lasted for several years, and when it ended she went to stay with her father. She returned to court in 894 at Onshi's command and was involved with Fujiwara no Tokihira (871–909) and others. She also had a child by Emperor Uda around 896, but the child died young. In 907 Onshi died. Ise then fell in love with Prince Atsuyoshi (887–930), a relationship that lasted until the prince died, and produced a daughter, Nakatsukasa, who was also known as a poet (see Round 3). It is not known how much longer Ise lived. In addition to being one of the more important poets in the *Kokin wakashū*, she was highly regarded by later poets and is well represented in the *Shin-kokin wakashū*. Altogether, one hundred seventy-eight of her poems are in imperial anthologies.

This poem appears in the Love section of the *Kokin wakashū* with this headnote: "After she was estranged from Nakahira, with whom she had been intimate, she went to Yamato Province where her father was governor and sent this poem to Nakahira."[1] Ise takes on the persona of Miwa Mountain, a well-known site in Yamato Province and a Shinto deity. Her poem presumes knowledge of an anonymous poem:[2]

waga io wa	The hut where I live
Miwa no yamamoto	Is just below Mount Miwa.
koishiku wa	If you long for me
toburaikimase	Then please come here and visit—
sugi tateru kado	The gate where the cedars stand.

Nakahira is being invited not so much by Ise's poem as by the poem it indirectly cites. According to the collected poems of Ise, he replied:[3]

morokoshi no	Even if she hid
Yoshino no yama ni	On a Yoshino Mountain
komoru tomo	In far-off China
owamu hito ni	How could I remain behind
ware okureme ya	Apart from the one I love?

Yoshino Mountain is, like Miwa, a remote and sacred mountain in Japan where the devout could escape the world. "I would go anywhere," he says, "for one I loved." On its face this is a positive response, but it leaves open the possibility that Ise is not the loved one he would follow.

172

Miwa no yama
ika ni machimimu
toshi futomo
tazunuru hito mo
araji to omoeba

This Mount Miwa,
How can it keep on waiting?
When it knows that,
Though entire years might pass,
There would be no visitor

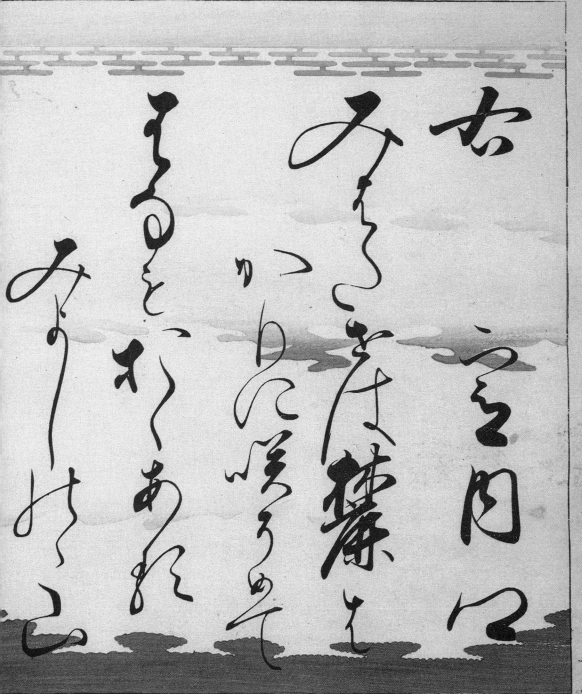

古今内ハ

みちて詞を

かりにいひ初めて

するをおそくあれ

みかりして己

小さやかに立花をを女十二冊末

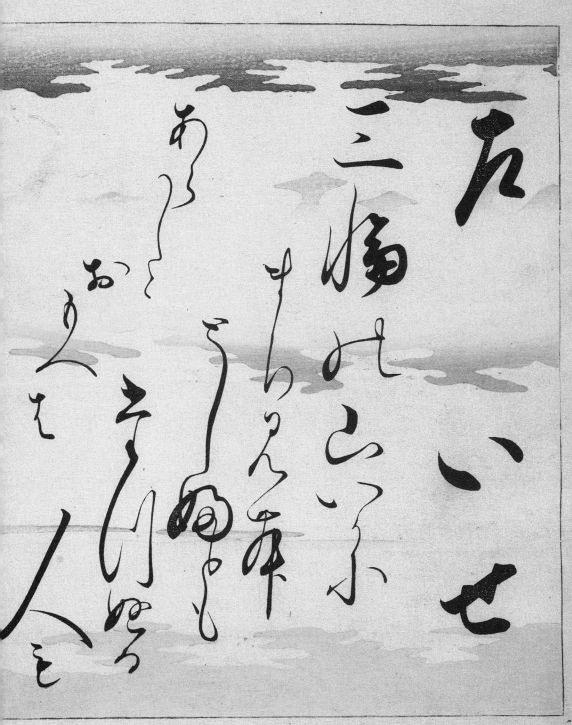

いせ

三輪やま
いかにまちみむ
としふとも
たつぬる
あひ
おり
人を

むら町　村田半平女八束書

1R / *Shikishi Naishinnō*

Shikishi Naishinnō, Princess Shikishi (1153?–1201), was the daughter of Emperor Goshirakawa (1127–1192; r. 1155–1158) and was the ceremonial Shinto priestess of Kamo Shrine for ten years during her childhood. She studied poetry under the greatest poet of the time, Fujiwara no Shunzei (1114–1204), and was seriously dedicated to the art. One hundred fifty-four of her poems were included in imperial anthologies. This poem is taken from the Love section of the *Shinkokin wakashū* and has this headnote: "On the subject of secret love, from a set of one hundred poems."[1]

As in Komachi's verse the poem describes longing at the beginning of an affair. But Princess Shikishi paradoxically uses language more commonly associated with the loss of love. The lady of the poem, caught up in her secret desire, is afraid she will forget that she is responsible for her own loneliness by not telling the man how she feels. Then she will be not like a woman in the beginning of love, but like a woman abandoned. No matter what she remembers or what she forgets, however, we expect that she will cry this evening out of a combination of loneliness, frustration, and desire.

The poem's convoluted reasoning is reinforced by its inverted grammatical structure. The last two lines are the object of "forget," and reading this correctly requires an act of memory analogous to the one described by the lady. The key word in the poem, *unchinagekaruru*, is based on the verb *nageku*, "to grieve," but with prefixes and suffixes added to make the action sharp and spontaneous and to have the word mimic the sound of sobbing. The poem remains fundamentally difficult to read because its deeper subject is the lady's struggle for self-awareness, the to-and-fro among memory, longing, anticipation, frustration, and fear. The poem resists reduction to the standard emotions of love poetry, such as resentment, loneliness, anger, or despair.

These first two poems have been carefully selected by the compiler, not as the best examples of the poets' work, but as part of the message of the competition as a whole. Komachi and Shikishi are the leaders of their two teams. Komachi is the great woman poet of the first period of court poetry, the eighth to tenth centuries, and Shikishi is the most prominent in the second period, the eleventh to thirteenth centuries. Shikishi's poem is more elegant in tone and more consciously artistic than Komachi's, indicating the mature sophistication of the poetic tradition in the second period. Komachi confronts desire directly, even satisfying it in a dream, while Shikishi uses love as the opportunity to expose consciousness.

In the imaginary portrait, Princess Shikishi is shown seated on a tatami mat behind a screen of state, as is the only other royal poet in the competition, Saigū no nyōgo (see Round 4), out of respect for their rank and high birth.

wasurete wa

unchinagekaruru

yūbe kana

ware nomi shirite

suguru tsukihi o

If I forget, oh,
How I will have to weep
When evening comes!
That months have passed
While I alone knew

1L / *Ono no Komachi*

Ono no Komachi is a popular subject of legend, but few facts about her life are known except that she was active at court in the middle of the ninth century.

She is the most famous of all Japanese women poets because her poetry is often especially complex and passionate, and because she was one of six poets, and the only woman, mentioned by name in the early-tenth-century preface to the *Kokin wakashū*. This preface was the first influential essay on poetry criticism, and these six became known as the *Rokkasen*, "The Six Immortal Poets." Only the eighteen poems by her in the *Kokin wakashū* can definitely be accepted as her compositions.

This poem was included in the *Kokin wakashū* without any headnote identifying the circumstances of its composition.[1] It does not show the complexity and intensity of language that make many of her poems so striking for contemporary readers, but it was very highly regarded in the Heian period (794–1185) as an expression of deep emotion, for it describes subjectivity so extreme that the distinction between reality and dream collapses.

Readers of the time would have recognized the situation of the speaker immediately, and would have enlarged upon the implicit narrative. A woman feels strongly attracted to a man, but because of the social restrictions on women of the nobility, she must wait until he comes to her. Her longing intensifies to the point that he appears in her dreams. A momentary joy, rare in Japanese love poetry, suddenly turns into the more familiar sense of frustration and loss.

The opening lines closely echo an earlier poem sent by an exiled courtier, Nakatomi no Yakamori (mid–eighth century), to his wife. The association with this well-known poem adds to Komachi's poem the suggestion of forced separation:[2]

omoitsutsu	Without fail
nureba ka moto na	Because I fall asleep
nubatama no	Longing for you
hitoyo mo ochizu	Every seed-black night
ime ni miyuru	You come to me in my dreams

Unlike Yakamori's poem, however, Komachi's verse is written as if it were for her alone, and through it we feel that we are given brief entry to her interior life.

omoitsutsu
nureba ya hito no
mietsuramu
yume to shiriseba
samezaramashi o

Did he come to me
Because I fell asleep
Longing for him?
If I had known it was a dream,
I would never have awakened!

1ʀ / *Shikishi Naishinnō*

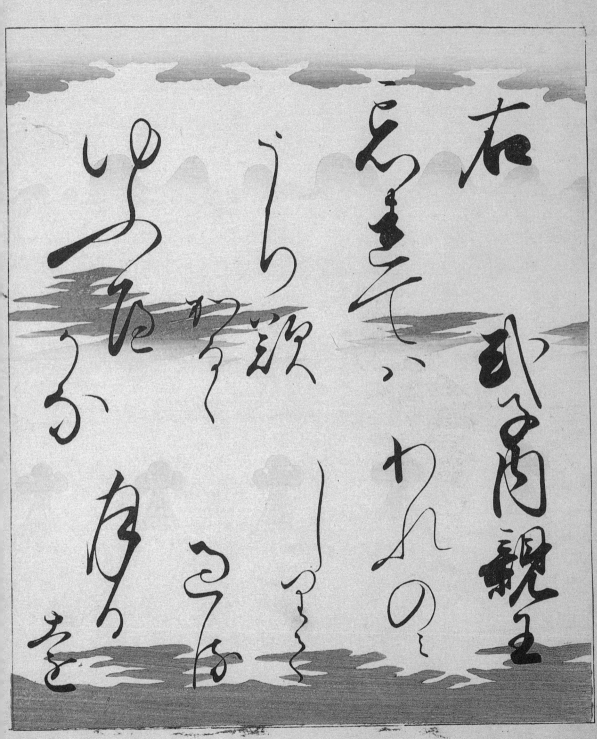

1ʟ / *Ono no Komachi*

左　　小野小町

はなのいろは

うつりにけりな

いたつらに

わかみよにふる

なかめせしまに

宗佐美枝廿七景書

Preface by Tachibana no Chikage[1]

Awaiting the flourishing of those blossoms that suit the name of Naniwazu,[2] he wishes to raise children with feelings that are not shallow as Mount Shallow,[3] but what he must teach are precisely those activities that are beyond learning.

This competition of the Thirty-six Immortal Women Poets has been recorded by young girls from the ages of six to fifteen who study with Mr. Hanagata and is accompanied by drawings by Mr. Hosoi[4] to form a work that seems more lovely than a cherry tree.

Although the calligraphy is so fine that some might doubt that such children could really have written this themselves, it is definitely the case that each one truly wrote in her own hand. All of these young girls, studying under their master, and wanting to follow what he taught, are able to form the shapes of the characters with surprising skill.

Tachibana no Chikage has written this preface to demonstrate that the flourishing of these blossoms is beyond doubt, and that the mountain well will not run dry.[5]

1. This preface no longer survives in the Spencer Collection album. The text for this translation has been taken from the version in the Chester Beatty Library in Dublin.

Tachibana no Chikage (1735–1808) was a major poet, calligrapher, and scholar of his time. As a poet he followed the mainstream court poetry style established by imperial anthologies such as the *Kokin wakashū* and *Shinkokin wakashū*. As a calligrapher he created his own distinctive style of the *kana* script. And as a scholar he is best known for his thirty-volume commentary on the *Man'yōshū*.

2. This phrase is an elegant reference to a famous poem cited in the preface to the *Kokin wakashū*:

Naniwazu ni	At Naniwazu
saku ya kono hana	How they bloom!
fuyugomori	These blossoms on the trees
ima wa harube to	Hidden through the winter,
sakuya kono hana	They tell us that spring has come.
	How they bloom!
	These blossoms on the trees

The poem was included in the preface as an example of a poem that seems to be about one thing (spring blossoms), but is actually about another (the long-awaited accession of Emperor Nintoku). There are at least two reasons why Chikage uses this reference: 1) he would like to suggest that the girls who recorded the poems in this book are blossoming young calligraphers; 2) this poem is traditionally the first practice poem for a child learning to write.

3. This phrase refers to MYS 3807, a poem from the *Man'yōshū* that is referred to in the *Kokin wakashū* preface. It was also used to teach calligraphy, and the *Kokin wakashū* preface calls this poem and the Naniwazu poem "the father and mother of poetry."

Asaka yama	Shallow is the mountain well
kage sae miyuru	Where only the reflection
yama no i no	Of Mount Shallow can be seen,
asaki kokoro o	And shallow would I be as well
waga omowanaku ni	If I were to feel no longing

4. Oddly enough the family name of the artist Hosoda Eishi is mistakenly recorded as Hosoi every time he is cited in this album—once in Chikage's preface, once in Hanagata Yoshiakira's afterword, and again in the colophon—too often to be a mistake. According to Klaus J. Brandt, Eishi deliberately avoided using his correct (and illustrious) family name to prevent it from being associated with a printed book. (See Klaus J. Brandt, *Hosoda Eishi 1756–1829: Der Japanische Maler und Holzschnittmeister und seine Schuler* (Stuttgart: K. J. Brandt, 1977), p. 165. The colophon, like the preface, is missing from the Spencer Collection text.

5. In this final line Chikage reintroduces his initial metaphors, based on the two ancient poems, of the spring blossoms and the deep well, to refer now to the budding students and their master as well as to the brilliance and depth of the poetic tradition as a whole. This flowery language itself imitates the style of prefaces to poetry anthologies.

The Frontispiece

The first illustration in this book is a print signed "Drawn by the artist Hokusai." Hokusai (1760–1849) is the grand master of Japanese printmaking, and the inclusion of one of his works adds interest and importance to the album for us as it must have for the original audience. But the relationship between the subject of the print and the album is obscure.

Three gentlemen, in the lower right corner, have just crossed a plank bridge on their way down from the hills toward their mansion in the upper left. It is spring and the cherry blossoms are in bloom. Although the men are dressed in court robes, their pant legs are rolled up and they are wearing simple sandals. I think that these three are poets who have been in the hills composing poetry and drinking among the mountain cherry blossoms. The poet in green is inebriated, and steadies himself with his right hand as he holds his spinning head with his left. The other two are deep in discussion, probably arguing some literary point.

Four retainers follow behind carrying the picnic gear, a folded umbrella, and a poet's son. Three farmboys, who are supposed to be gathering something in the hills, laugh derisively at the drunken poets.

If Hokusai designed this print specifically as the frontispiece for the album, one cannot help but wonder whether the calligraphy teachers were disappointed. It is an attractive enough picture, but it is a sharp jibe at both court poetry and calligraphy by children, and is completely out of step with the reverent tone of the book.

The Heian nobility were described as "those who live above the clouds," as this picture suggests literally by the band of cloud around the mansion. But these poets are comical figures, drunk on wine as much as verse, following in an ancient literary tradition of intoxication in the mountains. We are meant to identify more with the farmboys than with the poets, and it seems as hard to imagine emulating the poets' effete ways as it is to conceive of the tired little boy as their skilled scribe.

If Hokusai meant this print as a wicked criticism of the album's enterprise, he at least softened the blow by making both the poets and the child male, so that there could be some question as to whether, in fact, the scene applies at all to the album.[1]

1. Hokusai created illustrations of both the Six Immortal Poets (in 1802 and 1810) and Teika's anthology *One Hundred Poems by One Hundred Poets* (begun in 1835). The *One Hundred Poems* series is illustrated and discussed in Peter Morse, *Hokusai: One Hundred Poets* (New York: George Braziller, 1989). It was commissioned by the same publisher who issued this album. These works suggest that Hokusai was sympathetic to court poetry in general, so it is difficult to account for the inappropriate character of this frontispiece. Perhaps Hokusai was obliged by his publisher to make this print despite his personal dislike for someone at the calligraphy school.

Hokusai

The Poets

Round 1
Left Team: Ono no Komachi (active, late ninth to early tenth century)
Right Team: Shikishi Naishinnō (1153?–1201)

Round 2
Left Team: Ise (active, late ninth to early tenth century)
Right Team: Kunaikyō (active, 1200–1204)

Round 3
Left Team: Nakatsukasa (active, mid- to late tenth century)
Right Team: Suō no naishi (active, late eleventh to early twelfth century)

Round 4
Left Team: Saigū no nyōgo (929–985)
Right Team: Shunzei no musume (1171?–1254)

Round 5
Left Team: Ukon (active, mid-tenth century)
Right Team: Taikenmon-in no Horikawa (active, early to mid-twelfth century)

Round 6
Left Team: Michitsuna no haha (ca. 936–995)
Right Team: Gishūmon-in no Tango (active, late twelfth to early thirteenth century)

Round 7
Left Team: Uma no naishi (active late tenth century)
Right Team: Kayōmon-in no Echizen (active, early to mid-thirteenth century)

Round 8
Left Team: Akazome Emon (ca. 957–1041?)
Right Team: Nijō-in no Sanuki (1141–1217)

Round 9
Left Team: Izumi Shikibu (ca. 975–1027–?)
Right Team: Kojijū (active, 1150–1200)

Round 10
Left Team: Kodai no Kimi (active, late tenth to early eleventh century)
Right Team: Gotoba-in no Shimotsuke (active, ca. 1204–1251)

Round 11

Left Team: Murasaki Shikibu (ca. 973–1014?)

Right Team: Ben no naishi (active, mid-thirteenth century)

Round 12

Left Team: Koshikibu no naishi (ca. 999–1025)

Right Team: Gofukakusa-in no shōshō no naishi (active, mid-thirteenth century)

Round 13

Left Team: Ise no tayū (active, ca. 1008–1060)

Right Team: Inpumon-in no tayū (active, mid- to late twelfth century)

Round 14

Left Team: Sei Shōnagon (966?–1010–?)

Right Team: Tsuchimikado-in no kozaishō (active, early thirteenth century)

Round 15

Left Team: Daini no sanmi (999–1078–?)

Right Team: Hachijō-in Takakura (active, late twelfth to early thirteenth century)

Round 16

Left Team: Gidōsanshi no haha (active, late tenth century)

Right Team: Gosaga-in Chūnagon no tenji (active, mid-thirteenth century)

Round 17

Left Team: Ichinomiya Kii (active, late eleventh to early twelfth century)

Right Team: Shikikenmon-in no Mikushige (active, mid-thirteenth century)

Round 18

Left Team: Sagami (active, ca. 1020–1060)

Right Team: Sōhekimon-in no shōshō (active, mid-thirteenth century)

The Album of
The Thirty-six Immortal Women Poets

This page marks the beginning of the 'Far Eastern-style' section of the volume.

Please note also that, in reproducing Eishi's album, we have followed the traditional format of the Japanese poetry competition, which groups the poets into "Rounds" and "Teams." For example, Ono no Komachi and Shikishi Naishinnō compete in Round One, and represent the Left Team (1L) and the Right Team (1R) respectively. Consequently, we have reproduced the imaginary portrait of Komachi on page 184, her poem on page 185, and the imaginary portrait of Shikishi on page 182, her poem on page 183. The commentary and translations that pertain to Komachi fall on pages 180 and 181, and the commentary and translations that pertain to Shikishi fall on pages 178 and 179.

Their Round is followed by the poets of Round Two, Ise on the Left Team (2L), and Kunaikyō on the Right Team (2R). This pattern continues through the last pair of poets in Round Eighteen, until all of the Thirty-six Immortal Women Poets have performed in the competition.